*Twayne's United States Authors Series*

Sylvia E. Bowman, *Editor*

INDIANA UNIVERSITY

*Mary Hunter Austin*

# MARY HUNTER AUSTIN

by T. M. PEARCE
University of New Mexico

 92

Twayne Publishers, Inc. :: New York

MANUFACTURED IN THE UNITED STATES OF AMERICA BY
UNITED PRINTING SERVICES, INC.
NEW HAVEN, CONN.

For
Helen

# Preface

MARY HUNTER AUSTIN has suffered perhaps as much from the diversity of her talents as from her failure to make a sensational success in the exercise of any one of them. Essayist, poet, novelist, lecturer, short-story writer, naturist, always the artist in image and word, essentially the propagandist in the use of both, she wrote thirty-five books and hundreds of shorter productions, all of which kept her before the reading public for a period of forty-two years. Her first story was published by the *Overland Monthly* in San Francisco in 1892. The last two of her books, *One-Smoke Stories* and *Can Prayer Be Answered*, appeared in the year of her death, 1934. How does one judge the impact of a writer through nearly half a century? When was the peak of her fame? Did it rise and then decline? Was it cumulative? Is it still growing? Was her achievement a permanent contribution to the literature of America?

Such evaluations do not depend upon the judgment of a single critic, but upon the opinions of many. The comments of both kindred and contrary spirits should go into the appraisal. Friend and foe alike make up a judgment "in the round," and the present writer will try to draw such a portrait: to show Mary Austin in depth, as it were. The pretty rotogravure print is easily made up. The lines and shadows of personal struggle should show in the portrait when they lend dignity and meaning.

In 1939, five years after Mrs. Austin's death, Helen Mac-Knight Doyle wrote *Mary Austin, Woman of Genius*. In the following year, I published *The Beloved House*. Dr. Dudley Taylor Wynn completed a dissertation in 1941 which was entitled *A Critical Study of the Writings of Mary Hunter Austin*. Then the Laboratory of Anthropology at Santa Fe, New Mexico, sponsored an evening of testimonials on September 1, 1944. At this time, some fourteen people contributed appreciations, some in person and others *in absentia*. Among the tributes read *in absentia* were those by Henry Seidel Canby and Carl Van

Doren. Upon these and other published materials, especially Mrs. Austin's autobiography *Earth Horizon,* I have drawn freely in the writing of this book. If at any time I have failed to acknowledge a specific indebtedness, the oversight is accidental, not intentional.

Any study of a writer must limit its objectives. This biography and critical analysis of Mrs. Austin's work will be divided as follows: the period of her youth spent in Illinois, the beginning of her writing career in California, the middle era of professional success in New York City, and the fulfillment of both her writing and social programs in New Mexico. This division and statement does not define the last years as the peak of Mary Austin's literary achievement. She may have left her mark as a writer in the studies of the Mojave Desert and the arid upland world of the California sierras.

The biography of Mary Austin should read like one of her novels, since her story is as dramatic as anything she imagined: the career of a girl born in a small town in a nineteenth-century Midwestern farming district who moved to the arid waste lands of the Pacific Coast and then found professional success in Europe and the complex metropolitan world of the Eastern seaboard, only to return to the environment of the village in an art colony of the Indian and Spanish Southwest. Throughout the years she describes herself as living two lives: the everyday life of Mary-by-Herself and the imaginary world of the writer I-Mary.

In both personalities she was always an active force, never just the observer recording only what she saw. Consequently, she left a record of both the American scene and of the forces moving in that landscape: those of harmony and those of conflict. Both in articles and in books, Mary Austin left a constructive statement. Perhaps this is represented in the name she chose for her residence in Santa Fe: *La Casa Querida,* "The Beloved House." Her total environment became a house beloved, a place enclosed by the environment of strength from the outer forces in nature; a space in which to look for creative contacts in people, places, and activities. Perhaps the reader will find her search as interesting and rewarding as she did.

I wish to acknowledge an especial debt to Jack Schaefer, outstanding Western writer now living in Santa Fe, who made

available to me materials from his "Mary Austin Collection."
Without them an appreciable amount of the bibliography would
be incomplete and the store of information depleted. So far as
I know, he has the finest Austiniana available anywhere. Harriet
Stoddard, Department of English, Blackburn College, has again
been of invaluable help in details relating to Carlinville, her
home as well as Mary Hunter Austin's. Donald P. Ringler, of
Bakersfield, checked the California days of the Hunter family
against his own extensive research into this period.

I knew Mary Austin for just four years. She was generous with
counsel during the founding years of *The New Mexico Quarterly*,
for which I was the first official editor. Wearing a Spanish
shawl and Indian jewelry, as she often did, she carried something of her imagined worlds around with her. The impression
remains with me still.

T. M. PEARCE

*The University of New Mexico*
*January, 1965*

# Contents

# Chronology

1868    Mary Hunter Austin born in Carlinville, Illinois, on September 9, 1868, the second daughter of Captain George Hunter and Susannah Savilla (Graham) Hunter. Mary had an older brother, James Milo, born in 1866. The first daughter, Hannah, born early in 1863, died a few months later. The family lived in a house on First South Street. Birth of sister Jennie, 1870.

1871    Moved to a farm at the edge of town where the psychic experience of "God and the Walnut Tree" occurred. Attended public school in Carlinville. Birth of brother George, 1876.

1878    Death of Captain Hunter; widow's pension supports family. Death of Mary's sister Jennie, "the only one who ever unselfishly loved me."

1884    Mary enrolls in Blackburn College, Carlinville; attends State Normal School, Bloomington, 1885; receives diploma from Blackburn, 1888.

1888    Susie, Jim, and Mary Hunter file on homestead land in Tejon district at south end of Joaquin Valley, California; Mary teaches school at Mountain View, 1889. Friendship with General Edward Fitzgerald Beale, owner of Rancho Tejon.

1891    Marriage to Stafford Austin, vineyardist, May 18, 1891; husband manages irrigation project in Owens Valley; failure of the project. Wallace Austin teaches school at Lone Pine.

1892    Birth of daughter Ruth. First story accepted by *Overland Monthly*, San Francisco. Mary teaches at the Academy in Bishop, 1895-1897. Association with Dr. Helen Mac-Knight, later Mrs. Doyle, who becomes the consultant for the baby, Ruth.

1896   Death of her mother. Wallace in 1896 and Mary in 1897
       teach at Lone Pine. Wallace becomes County Super-
       intendent of Schools, 1898; Registrar of Land Office at
       Independence, 1899. Mary goes to Los Angeles; meets
       Charles F. Lummis and his literary circle; teaches at
       the Normal School in 1899.

1900   Returns to Independence, where she builds "the brown
       house under the willow tree." Sells stories to *Atlantic
       Monthly, Cosmopolitan, St. Nicholas*. Daughter Ruth is
       placed with a family and later in a private institution for
       the mentally retarded.

1903   Publication of *The Land of Little Rain* (Boston and
       New York).

1904   George Sterling, Mary Austin, and Jack London in
       residence at Carmel, California. Publication of *The Basket
       Woman* (Boston and New York). The *literati* who came
       to Carmel or lived nearby: Jack London, George Sterling,
       Harry Leon Wilson, Charles Warren Stoddard, Ambrose
       Bierce, John Muir, Edwin Markham, Michael Williams,
       James M. Hopper.

1905   Writing at Carmel. Her novel *Isidro* published (Boston,
       New York).

1906   Destruction of the Owens River Valley by the Los
       Angeles Water District. *The Flock* (Boston, New York).
       Estrangement from Wallace Austin. The San Francisco
       fire. Ray Stannard Baker, Lincoln Steffens, and others
       join the Carmel group.

1908   *Santa Lucia* (New York, London). The Italian trip:
       background for *Christ in Italy*, not published until 1911.

1909   *Lost Borders* appears during her London visit. In Eng-
       land she joins the Herbert Hoovers; meets H. G. Wells,
       Hilaire Belloc, Bernard Shaw, Henry James, William
       Butler Yeats, the Joseph Conrads.

1910   *Outland* (London), published under the pseudonym
       Gordon Stairs. Republished (New York, 1919).

1911   Production of *The Arrow Maker* in New York City, by
       the New Theater, under the direction of George Foster

Platt. Published the same year (New York). Return to Carmel.

1912  *A Woman of Genius* (New York). Reissued, 1917 (Boston, New York). Enlists in feminist causes in New York with Anna Howard Shaw, Charlotte Perkins Gilman, Elizabeth Gurley Flynn, Margaret Sanger, Anne Martin.

1913  *The Lovely Lady* (New York). *The Green Bough, A Tale of the Resurrection* (New York). *Love and the Soul Maker* (Boston, New York). Mary's second Indian play "Fire" is produced at the Forest Theater, Carmel: "There was beauty and strangeness to the life at Carmel; beauty of a Greek quality, but not too Greek; 'green fires and billows tremulous with light.'" Mary joins the New York salon of Mabel Dodge, later Luhan of Taos.

1914  Death in a sanatorium of daughter Ruth. *California, Land of the Sun* (London). Reissued in 1927 (New York). Divorced by Stafford Wallace Austin at San Bernardino, California, August 21.

1915  *The Man Jesus* (New York). Reissued in 1925 as *A Small Town Man*. Mary undertakes the Eastern publicity campaign for the Panama-Pacific Exposition.

1917  *The Ford* (Boston, New York). Life alternates between New York and California, with Mary's pen at work on Riverside Drive, at National Arts Club, and in the wickiup behind her house at Carmel.

1920  *26 Jayne Street* (Boston, New York): "Somehow, Madelon, all women that interest me most in America have been unhappy. With men, I mean. Maybe it was so abroad— there was Duse——"

1922  Second trip to England to lecture before the Fabian Society.

1924  Mary Austin decides to move to Santa Fe: study of Indian poetry and Spanish folk culture. *The American Rhythm* (Boston, New York): "Almost anybody might have predicted the rise of a new verse form in America." *The Land of Journeys' Ending* (London): "Between the Rio Colorado and the upper course of the Rio Grande lies the land of Journeys' ending."

1925  Building of her home, Casa Querida, in Santa Fe.

1927  Organization of Spanish Arts Society in Santa Fe.

1928  *The Children Sing in the Far West* (Boston, New York).

1930  *The American Rhythm.* Second Edition (Boston, New York).

1931  *Experiences Facing Death* (Indianapolis): "Death may yet be demonstrated... to be of the nature of a link in experience rather than its unavoidable end." *Starry Adventure* (Boston, New York).

1932  *Earth Horizon* (Boston, New York): the story of I-Mary in the words of Mary-by-Herself: "It is not that we work upon the Cosmos, but it works in us."

1934  *One Smoke Stories* (Boston, New York). *Can Prayer Be Answered?* (New York). Death in Santa Fe, August 13, 1934.

1937  Burial of her ashes on Mt. Picacho, east of Santa Fe, August 13, 1937.

# PART I: THE WOMAN

About this time Mary learned that a group of young people who called themselves the Fox Tail Rangers were on a camping party at El Tejon. She rode out to join them. . . . They rode off and left her alone in the camp. It was a cruel thing to do and they knew it. When they returned, they found Mary sitting on a rock near the bridge busy with her pad and pencil. They resented finding her absorbed and said among themselves that she had posed by the bridge and the pad and pencil were just to show how superior she felt.

—HELEN MacKNIGHT DOYLE

Everybody who talked with Mary Austin knew at once that there was greatness in her. What she may have been like in the days of her early ambitions I could never quite make out. She was past fifty when I first met her, and she seemed then to have been always wise and secure.

—CARL VAN DOREN

## CHAPTER 1

# The Youthful Mystic.
# Illinois, 1868-1884

AMERICANS ARE NOT a mystical people. As a generalization, that statement seems safe enough. Temperamentally, Americans have been extroverts, people with the practical sagacity to set goals in almost every field of human endeavor and to achieve them. One area, that of communion with realities beyond physical experience, has been neglected; that is, ultimate existence known by a personal and unique approach. Organized religious groups, in many rituals and doctrines, have brought spiritual kingdoms to individuals and groups throughout the United States on Sunday and every day in the week. This has been mystical communication through formula and creed, but in every faith exceptional individuals have found an Inner Light more intense than any statement or formula. Among the Society of Friends, better known as Quakers, mystical fellowship has been a way of worship. However, even here direct illumination is sought in the company of others, not in isolation as with most mystics. The Anglo-Saxon character, patriarchal and clan-minded, has from its earliest roots produced few individuals enraptured with solitude or bound to the cosmos.

That is why a Henry Thoreau, feeling the subtle magnetism in nature around Walden Pond, and a John Muir, contemplating what he calls the "predestined grandeur" of California's sierras, seem a bit peculiar and strange in the literary pantheon of this country. Something was carried to these men from the solitude of a lake or the austerity of a grove of trees, the grandeur of a granite cliff, the dome of space. They discovered purpose and intention in phenomena which to other people were only picturesque or benign when not threatening. To such company must be admitted a third American writer, one of the opposite sex, one to whom the communication from nature came at a much earlier age than it ordinarily comes to worshipers of natural phenomena.

## I Carlinville Beginnings

Mary Hunter was born in the small Illinois town of Carlinville on September 9, 1868. She arrived, according to her own statement, upon the "stroke of midnight." Whether her comment indicates that she knew that in astrology the midnight hour is in a House of Power and in universal folklore is the "witching hour," her reference to the striking of the midnight bell seems more than casual. She also records that the uncle who was present called her "the noticingest" baby he had ever seen.[1]

Mary's father, George Hunter, served during the Civil War with Carlinville's Company K of the Seventh Illinois Volunteers. The members of this Company christened themselves the "Macoupin Invincibles," for their home county of Macoupin. To her father, Mary traced the literary tendencies which were manifested in her at an early age. His love for books showed in his first editions of Keats and Shelley, Mrs. Browning and Ruskin, along with the editions of such notable Americans as Melville, Hawthorne, Poe, Longfellow, and Emerson. Before the Civil War, George Hunter read at law and opened an office above Milo Graham's drugstore in Carlinville. Enlisting with the first militia in April, 1861, he returned in August as Captain Hunter and married Susannah Savilla Graham, the daughter of his landlord. She went with him down the Mississippi to Fort Henry and Fort Donelson where he served in the army's legal division until the end of his enlistment.

The Hunters lost their first child during the war. Completing his term of service in 1864, Captain Hunter began to practice law again in Carlinville and built a small house on First South Street, not far from the old office. Here the next three Hunter children arrived: James Milo in 1866, Mary two years later, Jennie in 1870. To accommodate the growing family, Captain Hunter moved outside Carlinville, about a mile south of the square, to a site with a house and several acres of land. This was the Plum Street place near Rinaker's Hill, which sloped under a large walnut tree to a stream, then to level meadow land called the Bottoms. With every child the world consists of indoors and outdoors, but with few did outdoors become so important as it did to the girl Mary.

## II  *God and the Walnut Tree*

The wonderland to which Mary Austin escaped throughout her life began with Rinaker's Hill, named for a Carlinville family which owned the property in the neighborhood. In the hilly pastures stood hickory and walnut trees; beneath their branches were dewberries, wood ferns, crocus plants and violets. Here was Arcadia for the children to explore. They could plan venturesome pilgrimages to undiscovered spots along the creek and the Bottoms, wade in the water hunting for crawfish, or listen to the hum of insects and the calls of birds.[2]

Near the house was an orchard of fruit trees. When Mary Hunter was not yet six years old, she came from the house on a summer morning and walked through the orchard alone. Moving down the slope of the hill, she felt the wind across her forehead and became aware of one tall walnut tree which seemed to reach far into the immensity of the blue sky. Suddenly, after a moment of quietness, the earth and sky and tree and wind-blown grass came alive for the child in the midst of them, all in a pulsing light. There was a wild foxglove at the child's feet and a bee dozing about it, and she writes "To this day I can recall the swift inclusive awareness of each for the whole— I in them and they in me and all of us enclosed in a warm, lucent bubble of livingness. I remember the child looking everywhere for the sources of this happy wonder, and at last she questioned—'God?'—because it was the only awesome word she knew. Deep inside, like the murmurous swinging of a bell, she heard the answer, 'God, God?' . . ."[3]

Thirty years later, Mrs. Austin described this experience as the one abiding reality in her life, something "unalterable except in the abounding fullness and frequency of its occurrence." The moment returned to her, when she needed guidance. A Presence was beside her, not a personalized Presence but warmth and light, and after a moment a Voice, as there was the first time under the Walnut tree. This would happen in the midst of work, a tall white Presence at her shoulder, and the Voice saying, "Wait," "Go forward," "Trust this person or this occasion." She states that she never thought of the manifestation as a ghost or an angel, but only as a force, a source of energy.[4]

The physical or psychological reality of Mary Hunter Austin's "Voice" or "Presence" became a source of power. Before her writing career was finished, she gave the experience a variety of names: the Soul-Maker, the Friend, the Friend of the Soul of Man, Everyman's Genius, the Sacred Middle. Each of these terms describes a form of insight and understanding. They were not the personal possession of Mary Hunter Austin, however closely she identifies herself with them. Rather, she proclaims herself the clear channel enabling such a Voice and such a Presence to speak to anyone for the environment of woodland and stream, for the sky and earth of America, for the creatures and peoples in the land which she observed and loved.

If these statements seem intangibles, they can only be judged as they are applied to and illustrated by Mary Austin's words and activities. They must be checked against her deeds and accomplishments, against the career of a sometimes willful and unprepossessing child; an awkward, self-absorbed young woman; an assertive, sometimes imperious individual, who was also a good cook, an entertaining storyteller; and a champion of neglected causes and peoples. With the help of her Voices and other sources of strength, she became a writer both persuasive and skillful, whose prose style was praised as "absolute and flawless" by a distinguished critic and playwright.[5]

When Mary was just ten years of age, she lost both her father and her sister within the space of two months. George Hunter never fully recovered from the malarial infection he had contracted during the Civil War. In her autobiography, *Earth Horizon*, Mary recalls the painful sound of asthmatic coughing and the odor of lozenges burned to soothe his throat and lungs. On October 29, 1878, Captain Hunter died. Late in December of that year Mary's sister Jennie died of diphtheria. Mary Hunter's ties were closer to her father than they were to her mother, and her love for her sister was deeper than that for either brother. Of Jennie, she asserts, "She was the only one who ever unselfishly loved me."[6]

Several years after Captain Hunter's death, the Plum Street

farm was sold because the fatherless family could not operate it. Susannah Hunter now lived on the pension provided by the government to the widow of an army officer, and the Hunters moved back to town. She found a house with six rooms arranged in two rows, and with two coal fireplaces ornamented by imitation black marble mantelpieces. Folding doors separated the parlor from the livingroom, and Mrs. Hunter had the woodwork in these two front rooms "grained" to imitate natural and expensive hardwood.

### III  *I-Mary and Mary-by-Herself*

This was the Johnson Street house of Mary's college days. Before that she had attended the Carlinville public schools, elementary and higher grades. There are no reports from her teachers during these early years. Mary herself records that she was reading words when other children in the first grade were still learning the sounds and letters upon a blackboard; that she was reciting Tennyson before she knew what his poems were about; and that she preferred Ben Jonson's *Complete Works* that stood on her father's bookshelves to the *Works* of Burns and Shakespeare because the volumes were bound in red with a tracery of gold. She also discovered that there were two Mary Hunters in the schoolroom: one, the Mary that was studying her book and supposed to be doing her lessons; and the other, the Mary that sailed out the window and walked on a log high over the creek. The first girl was Mary-by-Herself, who did what had to be done where she was, the every-day Mary; the other girl was I-Mary, who did what she wanted to wherever she wanted to be; who stood apart observing and later writing what she saw, creating a different world in thought and deed. This separation divided the actual from the possible, and made a "real" world come alive in her mind, a place she could go if she didn't like the place where she was. It was also the world of stored-up experience from which her books came to be written later on.

Mary began her storytelling while sitting in the middle of a haymow on a summer afternoon, or on the rim of an old stone quarry where the audience dangled bare feet in the pools of water. Then there were fireside groups of children which had something in common later in her life with gatherings of Indians around adobe hearths, saying, "Now tell me a story" or "There was a telling." Young Mary had learned whole pages of *Hiawatha* by heart and could recite with elocutionary force. At the age of ten years, she composed "A Play To Be Sung." The combination of drama and music had been produced by her favorite reading, Lewis Carroll's *Alice in Wonderland;* but Mary had certainly never seen an opera and never heard of a story set to music.

## IV  *Blackburn College Days*

At Blackburn College, Mary Hunter selected a major in science despite the fact that one of her favorite professors had no faith in the new science of flying. This was not long before the Wright brothers lifted their first glider into the air at Kitty Hawk, North Carolina; but, if an instructor in the English Department at Blackburn had shown such lack of vision, Mary doubtless would have charged his deficiency to a mental flaw. She felt, of course, that she could teach English to herself, which is true of any field of knowledge depending upon the will and capacity of the student. She preferred science, but she practiced her English. She wrote a poem when General John A. Logan, a senator from Illinois, died in Washington after an illness of only a few days. The whole country was shocked by the suddenness of his death. The question developed as to whether he should be buried in Illinois where he was born, or in Washington where he had labored with such distinction. Representatives and senators from other states maintained that he was no longer a local but a national character, and his remains should be interred in the government cemetery at the national capital. Mary Hunter, who agreed with the Illinois sentiment, wrote the tribute published in *The Carlinville Democrat* on January 6, 1887. The title was "Bring Him Home" and the expression was stately and conventional:

> Bring him home, his life work ended,
> Lay him down to his last rest;
> Let no funeral pomp attend him,
> Simply, sadly, it is best.

> He will need no marble column,
> Punctured shaft or sculptured dome,
> In our hearts we'll write his praises
> When they bring our hero home.[7]

She was sufficiently reputed for literary talents to become the editor of her college journal and to be elected Class Poet, but science and mathematics (for which she admitted no talent whatsoever) were more stimulating to her imagination. She declares that even those propositions which she could only master sufficiently to make a possible recitation set up in her a spirituality, an awareness of space as one of the dimensions of reality. In the midst of problems but half apprehended "she would be seized with a sudden dazzle of the spirit . . . a sensibility for which there is no intelligible speech."[8]

Though honored by academic institutions across the land, Mary Hunter Austin was disposed to be critical of them. She refers to small colleges throughout the Midwest as those which have "undoubtedly played their part in determining the character of its culture and prescribing the limits of its intellectual assumptions," but despite their limitations she regrets that so many of them have been absorbed into the "vast caravansaries of book learning" which took their place. Blackburn College left her, she says, without "a thumbprint of predilection" so far as choosing a professional career; but this state she counted entirely to the good because she thereby escaped with a free intelligence and an unhampered use of herself.[9]

At this period of her life, Mary Hunter was, in her own words, "under the average height, not well filled out, with the slightly sallow pallor of the malaria country, with a tendency to bluish shadows under the eyes, and made to look older than she was by reason of the mass of tawney hair, brown with coppery glints, thick and springy, falling below her knees when loosed, and difficult to get under any sort of hat suitable to her years."[10] This self-portrait stresses the "crowning glory" of her hair while confessing to less attractive charms. When she had achieved a modicum of literary fame and was living at Carmel, California, in the artist colony which she helped to found, she had the habit of taking down her hair during studio parties and outdoor "get togethers." She must have felt more comfortable by freeing her hair, and she certainly displayed a feature to be admired. The poet George Sterling, however, got tired of seeing her go through this exercise, and on one occasion took off her shoes, as well, saying that "if she wanted to undress she might as well go the whole way."[11]

As for hats, Mary Austin and her hats became a legend to those who knew her. One of her friends who lived nearby after Mrs. Austin moved to Santa Fe described her hats as museum pieces of the Victorian age adapted from time to time to meet some notable modern trend. The size of the crown, of course, had to be conditioned to the expansive bulk of hair beneath. Some of the hats were big velvet ones with crushed crowns and floral ornaments, in one case, pansies. A straw hat with blue tulle around the edge and turquoise poppies on the side, tied by a ribbon of matching hue, made a lasting impression during several seasons of warm weather. Concentration upon the hat, in Mrs. Austin's case, may be partly symbolic. As a naturist, she believed in freeing soul and body from many social conventions. In her battle of the hat, Mary Austin presented all the determination to be as impressive as any of the other women, if not more so, while her contempt for the thing on her head fought with her pride in it.

The Blackburn College days brought men and matrimony into the foreground. Mary Hunter was especially drawn to a man who wore bright neckties and smoked cigars, but her mother disapproved of him and this discouragement was final. Since Blackburn had been founded by the Presbyterian Church as an institution to recruit and train young men for the ministry, the more eligible marriage prospects were future clergymen. They met with the hearty approval of Mary's mother. When one of them made Mary an offer, he did not arouse any particular response on her part; and she was faced with the problem of rejecting him without provoking resentment. The easiest way out seemed to be a disagreement about theology. Mary told him she could not marry a man who believed in Infant Damnation. Not even his reassurance that he would personally see that their children were immediately baptized could repair the damage. The young man wrote to her two days later withdrawing his proposal of marriage. Mary "kept company" with another ministerial student; but, despite their harmonious approach to theology, nothing matrimonial developed from the friendship.

## V  *The Move to California*

Brother Jim Hunter had finished at Blackburn two years before Mary. Although he enjoyed farming, he had been teaching for a year without any particular enthusiasm for this vocation. Letters came from Susie Hunter's cousin in California, encouraging Jim to come there and offering hospitality to all the Hunters if they migrated and filed for homesteads on government land. The promise of California appealed to Jim; and, with his mother's encouragement, he left for Pasadena. After his departure Susie Hunter could not stand the thought of separation from her oldest child. She arranged for a tenant to occupy the Carlinville house and then sold such of the household goods as she could do without. She shipped the rest to California.

Although this move enlarged the world of Mary Hunter, Mary disapproved of it thoroughly, opposing the break in her mother's life, the separation from relatives and friends. Susie would miss the many activities in her church. She would lack the minimum needs of her middle age. Susannah Hunter was forty-five years old when she led her family to the barren range-land of Tejon Pass bordering on the Mojave Desert. The pioneer impulse may have still survived in her. It certainly survived in her daughter.[12]

## CHAPTER 2

# The Voice of Nature.
# California, 1884-1912

TRAVELING WEST, the greatest experience that came to
Mary Hunter was her first sight of the desert, a vast space
unfolding before her from the Salt Lake Basin and stretching
to the Mojave lands beyond the horizon. Most of the passengers
on the train reacted quite differently to the empty space and
the silence. To them it was "God-forsaken, good-for-nothing."
It drew from Mary the anticipation of something expected,
something known. She felt pulled into this open world.

After a visit in San Francisco, the family took a cruise to
Monrovia, where James Hunter had found a job in a drugstore.
Reunited, all of them met relatives and friends from Illinois
in Los Angeles and Pasadena. Los Angeles was then in a form-
ative stage, as it seems perpetually to have been during the
last century. The old Spanish settlement was still recognizable
in its plaza with adobe buildings. The new American suburbs
were outlined with palms and eucalyptus, the streets pushing
ever outward. But in some places newly planted trees were
drying up; a real estate boom had just collapsed. The Carlin-
villians packed their camping equipment and provisions into
a wagon, harnessed the wagon horses while Mary mounted the
saddle horse, and the great homesteading adventure was
under way.[1]

### I  *The Homestead at Tejon Pass*

They were a week reaching their destination, three tracts of
180 acres each on high valley land at the beginning of Tejon
Pass south of Bakersfield. The railroad crossed the range to the
east of the homestead, and a vast cattle company owned by

General Edward Fitzgerald Beale spread over most of the Tejon area with its canyons and adjacent terrain. Many of the homesteaders, like the Hunters, came from wooded lands in the Midwest or from farther east. They had little knowledge of arid country. They built their cabins on the homesteads; plowed and planted the required number of acres; lived upon their savings until the rain failed to come, and then left to find jobs, returning only to "prove out" their claims. The Hunters moved once from their two cabins to an old stage-coach station nearer the Tejon Ranch store. Throughout the homesteading experience, Mary alternated between elation and despair.

Elation came when she rode out on her horse to witness community activities at the sheep and cattle ranches or in the Indian villages. On the pasture lands she watched the herders branding and shearing. The sheep dogs working the flocks fascinated her as did the signals between shepherds and the herding dogs. Later on she wrote an almost unbelievable account of how these dogs seemed to be able to follow a story when the words used were accompanied by gestures which helped to picture and communicate the perils from coyotes or other animals and from storms.[2] She observed the habits of the Spanish vaqueros and the American cowboys, even to the varieties of their camp cooking. Equally absorbing was the animal world, near or far from the presence of men: the cattle turning round and round until they kneeled to bed down; coyotes spelling one another in relays and running down a deer or an antelope; stallions guarding their brood mares; meadowlarks shading the eggs as the sun threatened to cook them before they could hatch; buzzards wheeling above dying animals in the tragic rhythm of life and death in a waterless pasture.

Despair came when drought killed off the cattle as the water-holes dried up, or when the homesteaders tossed grain into parched furrows only to watch gophers and kangaroo rats carrying the seeds to their own empty storehouses. Along with many others, the Hunter family gradually abandoned homesteading. Mary left after one year; Susie stayed until 1892; James until 1894. Susie bought a small farm near Bakersfield for Jim, George, and herself. Mary's independence had been asserted when she began to teach. She was appointed to the staff of one of the Kern County public schools during the fall of 1889, but after four months she stopped teaching because of illness. When she recovered, she started to give lessons as a private tutor to children in the homes around Mountain View Dairy, a farm settlement in irrigated country near Bakersfield. General Beale, who had become a kind of patron, took her to Indian villages where she learned of the Chisera or Medicine Woman she describes in her book *The Flock* and in her play *The Arrow Maker*. Beale helped many of the homesteaders by paying them for the right to graze cattle on their land.

In her autobiography, *Earth Horizon*, Mary Austin pays tribute to General Beale, the owner of Tejon Ranch. He seems to have combined the elements of executive efficiency and cultured intelligence which she most admired. As a lieutenant, Edward Fitzgerald Beale had served with General Kearney in 1846 when American forces occupied California. His attitude toward the Spanish-speaking settlers had been fair and civilized. He and Kit Carson crossed the continent together to carry the news of the conquest of California to Washington. In 1848, Beale reported to Washington the discovery of gold in California. Four years later he became the first superintendent of Indian affairs in this Western territory. He was also famed for the camel herd he imported when he was in charge of a survey from Ft. Defiance, New Mexico, to the Colorado River in Utah and Arizona. One of his men gave Mary Hunter a strand of Spanish hair rope that had been fastened to one of the camel bells. She later used it as a doorbell for the house she built at Carmel. One of her visitors reported that he entered Mary Austin's house by pulling on a cow's tail![3]

To the average person, nothing about the Tejon homestead could have been added to the credit side, considering the loss of time and money. To Mary Austin, the feel of the earth was slowly beginning to manifest itself. Even in the drought of the first April at Tejon, the mirages held a spell for her. Where the run-off of a brief rain had moistened the arroyos, blue lupins sprang up "as though pieces of the sky had fallen." Poppies came through the sandy soil, and the warm persuasive sweetness of her ultimate reality returned—that moment she felt as a child under the Walnut tree at Rinaker's Hill in Carlinville. She did not hear the word "God" in answer to her question, for this time she did not question. She knew that warmth and light, beauty and fullness are within all nature and that she had become a part of this totality. It was always there to participate in. She meant to share what she found.

## II  *Marriage to Stafford Wallace Austin*

In the summer of 1890, Mary Hunter became engaged to Stafford Wallace Austin, a gentleman-farmer-speculator who lived in the Owens River Valley near the settlement called Lone Pine. In 1890, he was raising grapes and alfalfa in the Mountain View Dairy area. Wallace Austin's brother, Frank, was in San Francisco trying to raise money to finance an irrigation ditch for the Owens Valley. The possibility of land sales, flourishing grape orchards, and other market produce loomed in the valley. In fact just such gardening as later was accomplished in the San Fernando and the San Bernardino regions from the water of Owens River and the Colorado could have been possible near Bishop and Lone Pine if the money had been found and if the engineers had gone to work.

On one of these business trips to San Francisco, Mary Austin took several of her stories to Ina Coolbrith, who had helped to edit and promote the *Overland Monthly* magazine. This periodical had been founded by Anton Roman, a San Francisco publisher and bookseller in the year of Mary Austin's birth.[4] The magazine had flourished in the 1860's, when Bret Harte was its editor and a regular contributor. With the passing of two decades, the *Overland* was still on its feet, but the days when the names of Charles Warren Stoddard, Ambrose Bierce, John Muir, Josiah Royce, and Henry George had flown at the masthead were past. Nevertheless, Mary Austin was justifiably proud when her story "The Mother of Felipe" appeared in the *Overland Monthly* in November, 1892.

Fifty-eight years after "The Mother of Felipe" was published, the Book Club of California reprinted it, along with four other earlier stories by Mrs. Austin. Rarely does a writer's early work compare favorably with his more mature production. Mrs. Austin's early poetry is inferior to her later verse, but her prose from the beginning will hold its own with the best in English or American literature. The same colorful picturing, the artistry in words, the fitness in rhythm and sound that relate the story

of the woman who refused to abandon her son to a desert grave
are found when Mary Austin writes the experiences of Gard
and Laura Sitwell in her last novel, *Starry Adventure.* The
relative merits of those shorter narratives and of her longer
stories will be considered in another chapter of this book.

When Frank Austin was not successful in financing the
Owens Valley irrigation company, Mary Austin's husband
floundered vainly and somewhat vaguely in the wake of his
brother's financial washout. Mary Austin tells how she became
chief assistant at a boardinghouse to tide her over the financial
insolvency of her first year of married bliss.[5] Publication of her
story in *The Overland* magazine held a lamp to her darkened
way, but with the birth of her daughter Ruth on October 30,
1892, Mary-of-the-warming-bottle and Mary-of-the-kitchen-stove
superseded Mary-of-the-writing-desk.

In the spring of 1893, Wallace Austin found a job teaching
at George's Creek in one of the district schools, and three years
later he took a position at Lone Pine where he became county
superintendent of schools in 1898 and 1899. During this time,
the Austins succumbed to the old homesteading lure and took
up a claim between Owens Lake and a series of rocky ridges
called the Alabama Hills. Since they were not pasturing cattle
or otherwise dependent upon the land for a living, Mary could
again explore the mysteries of the arroyos and record the
frontier ballads and the Spanish *canciones* she heard sung to
guitar accompaniment at the sociables in the mining camps.
On such occasions, Mary Hunter recited poetry and the camp
foreman performed card tricks; some of the Cornish miners
furnished country dances, and the activities often ended with
community singing.

Mary herself taught from 1895 to 1897 at the Methodist
Academy in Bishop, California, a town near the head of Owens
Valley. Then for two years she assisted her husband at Lone
Pine. The following year she went to Los Angeles, where she
had been invited to join the faculty at the Normal School. Dr.
Edward T. Pierce, head of the school, was a friend of Charles
Fletcher Lummis, who by this time had published nearly a
dozen books and was the editor of *Out West,* a magazine. The
Indian and Spanish past of California and the Southwest was
his chief field of investigation, as the titles of his better known

books disclose: *A New Mexico David* (1891), *The Land of Poco Tiempo* (1893), *The Spanish Pioneers* (1893), *The Man Who Married the Moon and Other Pueblo Indian Folk-Stories* (1894), *The King of the Broncos and Other Stories of New Mexico* (1897).

Although Mary Austin reveals that Lummis said that she had talent but no genius, he published a good many of her early writings between 1897 and 1904 and quite evidently his career offered almost a pilot program for her own. Furthermore, at the Lummis home she met the local writers. The best known members of the Los Angeles group were the poets Sharlott Hall and Edwin Markham; the anthropologist and historian, Frederick Webb Hodge; the reformer, poet, and lecturer, Charlotte Perkins Stetson (later Gilman), grandniece of Harriet Beecher Stowe and of Henry Ward Beecher; Grace Ellery Channing, also of a distinguished New England line, friend of Charlotte Perkins, and in love with her artist husband, Charles Walter Stetson whom she later married. When Grace Channing married Stetson and assumed mothering of Charlotte's child, the subsequent scandalous gossip was heard from the East Coast to the West.[6]

## III   Early Literary Successes

Two more of Mary Austin's stories appeared in *The Overland Monthly* in 1897, "The Wooing of the Señorita" and "The Conversion of Ah Lew Sing," which was reprinted in *One Smoke Stories* nearly four decades later. Then *Out West* began to take both poems and stories from her pen, and in July of 1900 the *Atlantic Monthly* published "Shepherd of the Sierras." In the next two years, her poems and stories were sold to *Munsey's Magazine, Cosmopolitan, St. Nicholas,* and *The Atlantic. Out West* continued to be a purchaser. Although editor Lummis could not pay so well as the big Eastern publications, nor command so large an audience, he could take pride in printing the early works of such writers as Jack London, Eugene Manlove Rhodes, Emerson Hough, Washington Matthews, Ernest Thompson Seton.

Moreover, one should not overlook Lummis' first-rate contributions to the history of the Spanish Missions and his widely read editorial commentary entitled "In the Lion's Den." Mary

Austin probably first heard from Charles Lummis of the pageantry of Indian dancing in New Mexico and of the variety of Spanish folk songs and native customs there. One of the distinguished members of the Lummis circle was David Starr Jordan, first president of Stanford University. He had a house at Carmel, and others of the Stanford faculty arrived during the early days of the colony. As a scientist, Jordan was especially interested in the geographic distribution of animals and plants in relation to their environment. Some of his environmental theories may have overlapped with the areas from which Mary Austin drew her own convictions of how nature shapes human societies.

Some writing situations come unsought to the favored few. Such an occasion brought Mary Austin to San Francisco during the severe earthquake and fire in April, 1906. She had gone to the Palace Hotel to meet her publishers, and she testifies that she felt oppressed by the atmosphere surrounding the hotel. She went so far as to call her brother George to tell him that the hotel was threatening to fall in upon her. She woke in the morning to discover that that was exactly what was happening. The roof was falling, furniture was crashing, chimneys were crumbling—all the noise and confusion of an earth temblor.[7] In the next year Dr. Jordan edited a volume describing the earthquake. A number of San Franciscans and others contributed their impressions of the temblor and subsequent holocaust, but Mary Austin wrote the most exciting version contained in the volume.

She begins her account: "Ours was a quiet neighborhood in the best times, undisturbed except by the hawker's cry or the seldom whistling hum of the wire; and in the two days following April eighteenth, it became a little lane out of Destruction." She pictures the lunging bureaus, the splitting doorframes, the exodus of people in bathrobes and kimonos, the waving palm trees. She writes that the dust of ruined walls had not settled before smoke darkened the sun and by nine o'clock the glowing disc showed bloodshot as the eye of Disaster. Odd details recurred to her, such as a potted geranium undisturbed on a window ledge when the brick veneer fell from the wall and the roof went through the flooring; an Italian woman kneeling in prayer on a street corner while the crowd trampled the bedding and clothing scattered beside her; a lodging house divided so cleanly that the rooms and halls looked like the burrows of an insect laid before a microscope. The crowd displayed moments of good nature and the ability to laugh at its own misery. She describes the rush to the park ahead of the flames on Market Street, the faces smudged and pallid and the figures bent forward under the rain of cinders. She summarizes by blaming most of the loss not upon the temblor, but upon the huddled buildings, the sinking foundations upon man-made ground, the weak frame towers and narrow streets. In her opinion, actual damage done by nature to the city was small beside damage made possible by human contrivance. The last impression she had of stricken San Francisco was when she left the desolate walls of the city and took the ferry to cross the bay to Oakland and Berkeley. As the ferry pulled out, the crowd gazed back upon a sign swinging in the wind. It carried the words: "Don't talk Earthquake. Talk Business."[8]

The glowing promise of Mary Austin's literary career found, however, no counterpart in her domestic life. The Austins at first placed their child with private families where she could have constant care. Then Ruth was sent to a mental institution at Santa Clara, California, where she lived to the age of twenty-two years. Grandmother Hunter viewed the child's mental disability as an act of God, pointing to it as a warning or a punishment: "I don't know what you've done daughter, to have such a judgment upon you."[9] The tragic irony is underlined when the woman physician who attended the child reported that Ruth had a beautiful face and lovely blonde hair. Physically she was well endowed, perfectly formed. Yet Dr. Doyle quotes Mary Austin as having said, "When I found I was going to have a child I wanted the smartest child that could be born; so I doubled my brain activity."[10]

All of the contributions Mary Austin sent to *Out West* are designated as from Independence, California, which was the county seat of Inyo County. She frequently refers to living at Inyo, when the reader expects her to say Lone Pine, the Alabama Hills, Bishop, or Independence, the town in Inyo County. She was at Independence from 1898 to the fall of 1905. In 1905 she built a house at Carmel on the rocky Pacific shore line five miles south of Monterey. Jack London was visiting there; Harry Leon Wilson had built a home farther out on the peninsula; and Charles Warren Stoddard was in Monterey. The success of her book, *The Land of Little Rain,* made the move to Carmel possible. She had not yet decided to end her marriage to Wallace Austin, but he remained in Independence.

## IV  *The Colony at Carmel*

Carlinville, Carmel, Santa Fe—all of these communities, whether in Illinois, California, or New Mexico—were small ones free from urban pressures and mass patterning. They were not the desert or homestead areas, but the next stage in social development: the stage at which social structure had emerged but not on a large and dominant scale. Despite Mary Austin's kinship to freedom in the wilderness and her disappointment with civilization as it had evolved, she never abandoned the human race to its selfishness and bad habits. She worked and fought for better beginnings and for better building in as many fields as she could find for her talents.[11] "You know, I think it is a great mistake for any artist to adhere exclusively to one mode of expression, and it is particularly bad for poets," she wrote to Arthur Davison Ficke; "because a gift for poetry is the one which fluctuates the most, and the creative centers ought to be kept alive."[12] Carmel bade fair to become a hospitable background for individual "creative centers." Mary Austin was, with Jack London, among the first writers to set up an establishment there.

Part of her establishment was a wickiup, a round structure made of poles and brush, like a Paiute Indian lodge. In this outdoor study, she placed her writing desk and captured an atmosphere appropriate to the world of Indian myth and legend. Her wickiup was not the only structure of interest at Carmel, for George Sterling had a sacred grove with a fireplace that looked like an altar, encircled by trees decorated with animal skulls. Sterling was said to resemble Dante in profile, with his Roman nose and forward-jutting brow; but Mary Austin wrote that Dante's squared face when viewed full front became thinned out in Sterling, whose mouth curled too much and whose jaw was less severe. She adds that Sterling would never, had he met his worst enemy in Hell, have kicked him in the face as

Dante did in *The Divine Comedy*. He would more likely have waited until the poor damned soul went by and then offered him a drink.[13] Robinson Jeffers, in later years paid tribute to "the great friendship and early fame" forged in the Carmel retreat.[14]

As might be anticipated, the separation between Wallace and Mary Austin grew wider after she went to Carmel, but an actual divorce did not occur until nine years later. Once she had left Independence for Carmel, she could never regain her former relationship with her husband. She tried to maintain an interest in his life at Inyo County, as evidenced by one experience they shared together: the destruction of the fruitful agricultural Owens Valley by the Metropolitan Water District of Los Angeles.

## V  *Owens River*

The United States Bureau of Reclamation began a survey of the Owens Valley as early as July, 1903. The engineers drew plans for dams and canals to irrigate two hundred thousand acres of valley land. At that time J. B. Lippincott, chief engineer of the Reclamation Service, was in charge of the survey. There were ten thousand people in the valley, and the little towns looked forward to their growth and future development. In 1904, a land company began to buy up the farming area along the Owens River and to purchase even the unimproved homestead claims. Head of the land company was a former mayor of Los Angeles. Within a few years, Los Angeles interests owned all the acreage along the Owens River, and with the land went the riparian water rights. At this time the Los Angeles Aqueduct Bill was introduced into Congress with the support of lobbyists interested in the San Fernando Valley. Mr. Lippincott resigned from the government service to work for the city of Los Angeles. Under the guidance of William Mulholland, chief of the Water Department, Los Angeles led the Owens River 275 miles into the urban water system. The Owens Valley was left to bake in the sun.[15]

On July 27, 1905, Stafford Wallace Austin, as Registrar of the Land office at Independence, wrote a protest to the Secretary of the Interior. On August 4, 1905, Austin wrote to President Theodore Roosevelt. To both men he pointed out the government's broken faith with the farmers. The President

did support an amendment to the bill limiting the water withdrawal to the domestic and civic needs of Los Angeles, but
the lobbyists interested in commercial agriculture near the city
won the support of Gifford Pinchot, then chief of the Division
of Forestry. The argument that farmers near a population center
needed water worse than farmers in the desert won out.[16]

The Austins took the defeat very much to heart: Wallace,
because he had worked for an irrigation company in the Valley;
Mary Austin, because this move struck a blow at her faith in
cultural evolution, the growth of people in harmony with
natural resources. A megalopolis like Los Angeles held no
greater promise for human fulfillment in Mary Austin's eyes
than a fruitful valley where farmers, vineyardists, cowboys,
sheepherders, ranchers, prospectors, and miners made a living
close to the soil. The rights of small communities matched
those of heavy industry and a moving picture colony. She
prophesied that, unless the city gave back the water, a time
would come when a great catastrophe would befall it. President
Franklin D. Roosevelt, at the dedication of Bonneville Dam,
some thirty years later, made much the same prediction when
he remarked that large cities can grow unhealthy if they destroy
the smaller communities of which they are the logical centers.
Their prosperity actually depends on the simultaneous healthy
growth of every smaller community within a radius of hundreds
of miles.[17]

When other sources of water, such as the Colorado River, were
put to use supplying the needs of Los Angeles and southern
California, some of the water in Owens River was returned to
the farmers there. The valley, however, never realized fully
the opportunities promised by the Reclamation Department
survey at the beginning of the century. Supporters of Los
Angeles point out that the city paid big prices for the Owens
Valley land, prices beyond the actual value. Mulholland, however, is quoted as having said that there were not enough
trees in Owens Valley to hang its people on.[18]

Sharing the depression felt by the people of the Owens
River country, Mary Austin knew that she would leave southern
California. Her work there seemed to be finished. She did not
return. Nevertheless, southern California had stored her mind
with the harvest of impressions and experiences that she wrote

into *The Land of Little Rain* and into *The Flock;* the settings and characters for her first two novels, *Isidro* and *Santa Lucia;* the vignettes of the desert places and desert dwellers found in *Lost Borders.* These riches were still with her, but there was need for a change of scene. She went to Europe.

## VI  *First European Tour*

England had previously welcomed a number of gifted writers from the West Coast. Bret Harte, Joaquin Miller, Ambrose Bierce, Charles Warren Stoddard, and others of the San Francisco *Overland Monthly* group had been frequenters of English literary circles two decades before Mary Austin arrived on the scene. Bret Harte had died in London just six years before she came there. Although Mark Twain was living in Connecticut, his reputation had been made in the Far West during the Virginia City days in Nevada. His lecture career was launched in California after his trip to the Sandwich Islands, the early name for Hawaii; and this trip had been arranged by the Sacramento *Union.* Mary Austin, of course, was in 1908 the first truly prominent woman writer from the American West. Her background and outlook were to be as stimulating to English listeners as those of her masculine Western predecessors.

She toured Italy before she went to London. Impressions of Christian art and the long pre-Christian era emerging into tradition appeared before her eyes in Italy and reappeared in her books *The Green Bough* and *Christ in Italy.* She felt herself the maverick, an independent who wanders away from the crowd. If this mood followed her to England, it did not show in her reception or behavior there. Perhaps this was because the Herbert Hoovers were, in a way, her hosts during the stay. She was with them on many occasions; they had been friends in California and knew that she was coming to London. Herbert Hoover drove her down to see the Joseph Conrads, for Mary was one of the few who had written Conrad from the United States. He said to her, "I stand on the shore and make my cry into the dark, and only now and then a cry comes back to me." He plucked a rose from the garden and handed it to her when she left.[19]

She met H. G. Wells and heard from his own lips the

domestic problem facing him. Mary Austin reported the conversation in the initial printing of *Earth Horizon;* but, upon the
protest of Wells, the lines were removed from the later copies
of the book. She attended the meetings of the Fabian Society
and talked with George Bernard Shaw. The Fabian Summer
School for this year was held during August at a large private
school in Surrey. Marie Stopes, author of *Married Love,* was one
of the lecturers; and Mary Austin not only lectured but also took
the leading part in a play she wrote called *Femina.* This was a
satire on the American Court of Domestic Relations which she
had loyally supported but which she also found a fit subject for
dramatic treatment. The English had no such institution, having
accepted as a corrective to their divorce laws, "the existence
in their midst of a class of professional correspondents." Mary
said the happy Fabians rocked with laughter at her play which
was given at the end of the week devoted to Women's Interests.[20] William Butler Yeats, she reported, told her that he
never read American poets. She picked up the interesting information from Mrs. Humphrey Ward that Americans had no
homes because all of them were divorced. Mary Austin came to
the conclusion that the English, however polite about their
hospitality, were not really interested in anybody else's ideas—
only in their own.

While in England, Mary Austin walked in some of the
suffragist parades. Her companion was Anne Martin, a young
American whom the Hoovers had known at Palo Alto. Anne
managed to get herself arrested in one of the London demonstrations, and Mr. Hoover had to bail her out. He was
annoyed because he thought American women should not get
themselves mixed up in England's problems.[21] These problems,
however, were not confined to England. Mary knew that they
were America's problems as well. When she returned to her
native land, she sought out its largest city with the biggest
problems to face. She had received a cable from William Archer
asking her to return to New York to produce her play *The
Arrow Maker.* There were difficulties when she arrived: the play
needed more sentiment, according to the director of the New
Theater group. Finally, the production came off with what
the author considered a success, and she returned to Carmel
to rest.

Yet the experience in the theater would not let her rest. She wrote another play about Indian life entitled *Fire*. This drama was produced in a natural amphitheater, and members of the Carmel Colony performed the roles in the cast. The author not only directed the production but also took part in it. The following summer, she presented *The Arrow Maker* for a second time. In the Carmel performance the wife of Harry Leon Wilson played the role of "Chisera," the Paiute Medicine Woman who was rejected by her tribe and then brought disaster upon it through the failure of her power. The Forest Theater is still the setting for the production of both experimental and professional plays.

Mary writes of the beauty and strangeness in the life at Carmel: "beauty of a Greek quality, but not too Greek; green fires and billows tremulous with light . . .; great teams from Sur, going by on the highroads with a sound of bells, and shadowy recesses within the wood, white with the droppings of night-haunting birds."[22] She published while in London a fantasy called *Outland*, dealing with a mysterious secret people inhabiting some such natural world as that found at Carmel. These were the Outliers; and on the edge of their retreat were the House-Folk, threatening to invade and destroy the Nature people. Although the author's sympathy was with the Outliers, her secret will was soon revealed when she left Carmel to return to New York City. She had decided to try her medicine—to exercise what magic she could summon upon the House-Folk of America's greatest city.

## CHAPTER 3

# The Small Town Rebel.
# New York, 1912-1924

"THE BLACKEST OF BLACK SHEEP to a Middle Western family" was the description Mary Austin once gave herself when reflecting upon her personal and literary past.[1] Overdramatic as the statement is, the words do emphasize an uphill fight to break away from many of the conventional attitudes and habits of thinking in her day. Her brother once took her aside, after she had been quoted as approving some modern socialized reform, and told her that, while the members of the family claimed no control over her opinions outside their house, they would not permit her to voice any such radical sentiments inside the family residence.[2] At a later time, Mary Austin commented that her grandfather was a radical Abolitionist in the period of slavery and that her mother was an intemperate Temperance advocate. Radicalism depends upon the point of view.[3]

During her stay in Europe, Mrs. Austin had met many professional women of letters who also lectured and even agitated for social reforms by means of public demonstrations in London streets. They supported programs calling for women's suffrage, greater economic and professional opportunities for women, child-labor laws, the legalizing of birth control, and the liberation of scientific knowledge about love and marriage. The English women were fighting for such progressive causes, and Mrs. Austin discovered that their counterparts were doing the same thing in many leading American cities. In New York, Mary lived for a time at the Washington Irving House on Riverside Drive; then she moved to the National Arts Club; finally to No. 10 Barrow Street in the Village. She seems to have been testing the climate in all parts of the city.

## I  A *Crusading Woman*

Probably no one could record what she was writing when she was at one place or another. The New York *Evening World* reported on November 8, 1912, that she considered a stingy husband a greater cause for divorce than an unfaithful one and that drunkenness and drug addiction were just as unjustifiable cruelty in marriage as infidelity. This was in an address to the women members of the New York Legislative League at a meeting in the Waldorf. Her recipe for happy marriages included instruction in the psychology of the sex relationship; the organization of marriage upon a financial basis, including a definite sum for the wife to use each week; and finally investigation of the forebears of each candidate to the marriage, so that data pertaining to mental or physical disabilities could be known and considered in the decision to wed or not to wed. She announced that she was writing a book on these matters. At the conclusion of her address, the league members gave their approval in a rising vote of applause.[4]

The book to which she referred was *Love and the Soul-Maker*. Published two years later, the volume becomes a lengthy dialogue between Valda McNath and Mary; and it expands the position that true love is a creative force governed by influences outside man. The urgency of physical passion is the same thing in mankind as the compulsion in animals, and propelling this force is the alternation of the seasons and the revolution of the planets about the sun. Grandiose though this concept may be, truth lies behind it. Mary, in the dialogue, points out how much higher the psychological structure is in human beings than in animals. This structure in married lovers serves an influence that is as creative as that which governs a great artist, shaping something beautiful, honest, and permanent. She calls this outer compulsion the Soul-Maker. Vague though the personification is, Mary Austin was not a hazy thinker. Her mind was logical and precise, but she expected a good deal of concentration from her readers.[5]

All of Mrs. Austin's time in New York City was not spent upon inquiries of such earnestness as *Love and the Soul-Maker*. World War I began on July 28, 1914, and not many months later Mrs. Austin was working on the Mayor's Committee for National

Defense, collecting food left on the docks or reclaimable at markets and preparing it at a community kitchen in City College Building on Twenty-third Street. She had already seen community kitchens in Montclair and Ossining, New York, where several barge loads of peas had been canned after they were declared unfit for market display. A faint but superficial mildew had formed upon them, and the owners were about ready to throw the cargo overboard.[6] The United States entered the war on April 6, 1917, and not long afterward Mary Austin suggested to the International Child Welfare League that children in the neighborhood of Public School No. 34 at Broome and Willet Street plant a war garden on vacant city land at Broadway and Mosholu Parkway. In August, a New York newspaper printed a picture of the boy farmers saluting Mrs. Austin in a garden of string beans, cucumbers, and squashes, after a special drill before their parents in which they carried American flags on their hoes. The gardeners earned hundreds of dollars besides helping to relieve the food shortage.[7]

Among the sponsors of literature and the arts during this period in New York City, none earned greater fame than Mabel Ganson Dodge who returned from Europe to New York in 1912 and moved to the General Sickles house at 23 Fifth Avenue. She had lived abroad for the previous ten years, and she and her husband Edwin Dodge had bought a villa in Florence where they entertained such notable figures as the great Italian actress Eleonora Duse, the English stage producer Gordon Craig, the American woman of letters Gertrude Stein, and many other famed personalities. For the next four years, Mabel Dodge held court in New York City, maintaining the nearest approach to a Paris salon to be found in America.[8] Among her many guests was Mary Austin who upon one of the "literary evenings" in 1913 was described by her hostess in the following words: "Mary Austin sat with her lips thrust out and her eyelids heavy, her gray hair coiled high, portentous in prairie-colored satin."[9]

During the New York years, Mary Austin wrote four novels, *A Woman of Genius, The Lovely Lady, The Ford,* and *No. 26 Jayne Street;* a play, *The Man Who Didn't Believe in Christmas;* a long narrative essay hitherto mentioned, *Love and the Soul Maker;* a psychological biography of Christ called *The Man Jesus;* a collection of animal stories, *The Trail Book;* and a collection of American Indian songs, first appearing in *The Forum* magazine and later in book form.[10] These twelve years, from 1812 through 1923, saw nine books written in the confines of New York's crowded precincts and thus became one of Mrs. Austin's most productive periods. Her play, *The Man Who Didn't Believe in Christmas,* was produced at the Cohan and Harris Theatre in 1916 and published in *St. Nicholas Magazine* the following year.[11] The cast consists of three groups of actors: The Real People (Alan, a lonely boy; Mr. Hardman, his father; and Mammy Delia, the housekeeper); The Passers-By (Grocer's Boy, Shopping Girl, Newsboy, and an Old Woman); The Story People (Red Riding Hood, Captain Kidd, Toby the Clown, the Three Bears, Fairy Princess, the Wizard of Oz, Dare-Devil Dick, the Indian Fighter, Clarice the World's Empress Bareback Rider). With a stage full of such pantomiming and glittering figures, no play had greater possibilities for success. The actors were as varied as the cast in Barrie's *Peter Pan,* but the plot was not so exciting as Wendy and Peter's battle with the pirates, nor were any two characters so dramatic as Tinker Bell and Captain Hook. Yet the reluctant father in Mary Austin's play relives his youth with all the vivid figures of storyland and comes, at last, to share his son's faith in them. Christmas returns to the boy's home at the same time.

## II   The Man Jesus

While Mary Austin was living in Greenwich Village, she undertook the most challenging task in her literary career: the book on the life of Jesus. She called it *A Small Town Man,* but the publishers advised against the title, doubtful that it would make the impression that a life of Jesus deserved to make. They chose the heading, *The Man Jesus.* Under this label the book appeared in 1915. However, when reissued in 1925, it bore the author's original caption. Here in the second largest city in the world was an author writing a book about a small-town individual. She was trying to find the Man of Nazareth, not the man in Christian art "so wan and womanish, so *elegant.*"[12] Nor did she find Jesus in the ritual and theology surrounding his life and writings. She sought the man who rose to fame among  a suppressed people who lived in the shadow of the mountains and who were divided into many factions by their feuds and by the topography of the land. Their common bond was the religious heritage and the deep-rutted tracks of Hebrew thought.[13] John the Baptist tried to unite these people by preaching of a kingdom at hand. His leader was a carpenter from Nazareth, who was a healer of men's bodies and a reader of their minds. Mrs. Austin points to these gifts as the fruits of the wilderness and the light of scriptures nourished in the small-town synagogues. Although the message of Jesus became universal, the lessons were learned in Nazareth, Capernaum, and Bethlehem. The truths which should make men free grew from insight into the life of the spirit, God power in man, man power approaching God.[14] The mystic fought to preserve the essence of divinity, but social pressures extinguished the light. Material forces clashing in mass conflict smothered the spark.

## III  *Attitude toward New York City*

Mary Austin resented New York despite the fact that she had no real cause to do so. The criticism of her books by reviewers there was almost invariably laudatory. She found the city absorbing and the people kind. New York was just too big to hold her interest. Furthermore, there were influences in a city of such size to which she was hostile. She says as much, beginning with the challenging remark that "the thing I suffered from worst in New York was boredom."[15] The immediate response to such a criticism of the largest, wealthiest, and most resplendent spot in the United States would be to find the critic deficient in wit or wisdom. Yet no one familiar with the mind of Mrs. Austin would make either comment. She continues to relate her opinions about New York: "I was bothered by the rage for success; the idea that an immediate success was the sign of capacity; that the little whorls of success that kept appearing on the surface of affairs were final and invincible." She complains of the insularity of viewpoint that New Yorkers had toward the world outside their city; their unwillingness to accept the idea that there might be anything going on somewhere else. Mary Austin might have documented her case by submitting a representative list of the great names in American art, literature, politics, and science with the places of birth, education, and production indicated. The overall view of American creative life is broader than that of any single center, one which might have circumscribed its criteria.[16]

Searching the American horizon for achievement drew Mary Austin into a lecture tour in 1921. She said that on this tour in the Midwest she discovered farmhouses with from one to five musical instruments, and in the Plains States there were music festivals, traveling art exhibits, and community theaters, ranging from playhouses to concrete Greek amphitheatres. The sale and circulation of books seemed to her below the other avenues of instruction and entertainment, but her survey convinced her that—whether in California, Texas, or Nebraska—there were both audiences of great variety and purchasing power, plus creative talent with the resources to express it.[17]

## IV  *The "Landscape Line"*

Basic to Mary Austin's rejection of any single group of critics or publishers as the shapers of American culture was her faith in the molding of all human effort by natural forces. To her, what a people make will resemble the things they look at most; the forms in the landscape will define the architecture that houses a people and its activities; these activities, based upon the resources in the land, will provide the pageantry and ceremonial customs for the work and recreation of peoples distributed across the surfaces of a country or confined within the boundaries of forest, water, hill and mountain heights. The "landscape line" is a phrase familiar to readers of Mary Austin's works, a concept embodying her total faith that men and their efforts are directed by an intention outside them which tries to guide them to a satisfying way of life.[18] She found the creative sources of Greek art and polity in the "keen peaks, round-breasted hills, and bloomy valleys" of the peninsula and the mainland of Greece. The Adriatic and the Aegean played their part in the city states of the Mediterranean shores; but so did the vineyards, the plowed fields, and the steaming oxen. In Mrs. Austin's hypothesis, the "great art-producing peoples have also been great agriculturists, much given to the joyous expression of their relation to the land they live in by green-corn dances, cherry-blossom fetes, and processions to Pomona."[19]

One can see why a rose tournament or an apple fair meant more to Mary Austin than a cocktail party, though she attended both, perhaps looking for traces of the "landscape line" wherever she found them.

Her confession as to why she left New York City and returned to the West is refreshingly honest. She felt more at home in an environment that was at once less complex and to her more interesting. The great metropolis was bemused by its own complexity; it missed the "open order of the country west of the Alleghenies." New Yorkers were intrigued with their own reactions and walled in by their own man-made heights of steel and mortar. She missed freshness, air, and light. Most of all, she could not discern the patterns or feel the roots. She was hungry for both feelings. She turned westward again.

## V  Move to New Mexico

But this time her turning did not lead to California. Mabel Dodge suggested a trip to New Mexico. Mrs. Dodge had divorced her architect husband, Edwin Dodge; and in 1917 she had married the sculptor Maurice Stern. They settled in New Mexico the following year. Mary Austin had planned to go to Mexico to write some magazine articles, and en route she decided to visit Mabel in Taos. Before going there, she stopped in Santa Fe. World War I had ended, and Mary celebrated the first Armistice Day by listening to the *mariachi* bands play in Santa Fe while she joined the crowds dancing in the streets. An epidemic had broken out in Mexico, and Mary lingered on in "the Land of Enchantment," as the New Mexico state slogan advertises. When she finally arrived in Taos, she was entertained along with others in the new literary salon Mabel Dodge Stern had established in a small replica of a Taos pueblo built by Mabel as the center of a small village which had twelve guest houses. She was soon to divorce Maurice Stern and to marry a handsome Taos Indian named Tony Luhan. With Mabel and Tony as guides, Mrs. Austin saw the Good Friday procession of the religious confraternity called *Los Hermanos Penitentes,* which re-enacts the trail of blood followed by Jesus Christ to Calvary. She saw the flagellation of the men bearing crosses and was reminded of the strange religious symbols of Italy.

Returning to Santa Fe from Taos, Mary Austin met a representative of the Carnegie Foundation and learned that in its Americanization program a survey was needed of the Spanish population and cultural institutions in Taos County. She carried out this investigation during the winter of 1917-1918; and then, in the following summer, she accompanied the well-known Santa Fe artist Gerald Cassidy and his wife on a sketching trip through the Rio Grande Valley and into the cactus country of southern Arizona, returning by way of the magnificent canyons of northern Arizona and the ancient pueblos of New Mexico. Both Cassidy and Austin sketched, the one with oil on canvas, the other with pencil on paper. From Mrs. Austin's notes came her *Land of Journeys' Ending*. She had selected the site of her next home: New Mexico.

In 1922, when erstwhile Fabian Mary Austin returned to her English friends to lecture at the summer school, she drove around the Shakespeare country with May Sinclair; met Marie Corelli, whose home in Stratford became the site of the Shakespeare Institute; and on one occasion at a Lyceum luncheon was invited by the chairman to say a few words "as a member of England's oldest colony."[20] She had lived in New York from 1922 to 1924, trying to learn the web of city life, the interweavings that form a pattern. She had worked as a typist; as a saleswoman; as a factory laborer; as a window-dresser. All of this pretending was to gather material for fiction about the city and the people shaped by the New York skyline and waterscapes. Finally she produced *No. 26 Jayne Street* incorporating some of this data. Her publishers considered the book definitely a failure.

An old horizon opened to her in Santa Fe: old, the community life of a small town set in a location of natural beauty. A new horizon opened as well: new, yet familiar from the Indian and Spanish contacts once glimpsed in California. The Paiutes and the Mojaves, however, never built such monuments as those at Chaco Canyon or at Aztec, New Mexico. The Spanish missions at Gran Quivira and Quarai antedated the California foundations by more than a hundred years, and the Indian-Spanish religious acculturation in the Pueblo Indian world offered richer soil for the investigator of primitive societies. Mary Austin felt that she could be useful in this world. She went there to find out if this was true.

CHAPTER *4*

# The Sage. New Mexico, 1924-1934

SANTA FE in 1924 was a city-village of less than ten thousand people. As the capital of the fourth largest region in the Union and as the political center of important cattle, mining, oil, and agricultural interests, Santa Fe deserved to be called a city. In fact, the political and religious authority of Santa Fe extended back to the beginning of the seventeenth century, and European contacts with the area pre-dated the city itself for almost a hundred years. An aura of culture and prestige lingered about the state and federal buildings, the historical and art museums, and the old Plaza with its monuments. The downtown section of Santa Fe had been in part re-platted in the nineteenth century as a conventional city, the streets surveyed and paved, the curbing and sidewalks lined up before red-brick houses with porches—all quite representative of any American community to the east or west. However, the city regimentation made no dent upon the roadways winding up the slope toward the foothills east of the Plaza, or those curving along the river and following the arroyos leading west to the Rio Grande. The new town that had grown up with the American occupation and the coming of the railroad still had old adobe houses built along the street lines and entered through *zaguans*, wide archways leading to patios and other rooms or buildings.

One of the well-known streets was named the Acequia Madre because of the big ditch that turned a water wheel to grind corn. A wandering *camino* that ran counter to it had been selected by a group of artists for their studios. They renamed the road *El Camino del Monte Sol*, "The road of the Sun Mountain." This was where Mary Austin selected a site for her new house, the first land she had owned since the days at Carmel. *La Casa*

*Querida* she called it, "The Beloved House"; and such it became, for here she could again plant the bushes and flowers that pleased her, the garden herbs that created aromas in the kitchen, the fruits that she used in her jams and jellies.

## I   *La Casa Querida: "The Beloved House"*

*La Casa Querida,* a wide adobe building with a broad terrace of brick facing north to the Sangre de Cristo mountain range, had ten rooms, including a big library-living room and a smaller study adjoining. Indian rugs covered the floors, and handmade tin light fixtures, carved tables, and Indian ollas both furnished and decorated the rooms. Paintings by Indian artists hung on the walls. The carved front door faced the Camino, and opened into a hall separating the study-library-dining room wing from the kitchen, and guest rooms on the south. Mary Austin's bedroom was next to her study on the north. An enclosed patio with an irregular kind of rose window filled in the space east of the dining room and a Spanish arbor or *ramada* surrounded the south side joining the service rooms to the garden. Here perhaps the two Mary's, the work-a-day Mary-by-Herself and the writer I-Mary, were at last most content, more nearly one and the same person.

To some people Mary Austin seemed to be a tall woman, but it was the mass of hair which she wrapped or rolled into a kind of crown on her head and lifted higher by the effect of a Spanish comb that made her seem tall. Perhaps her erect stature simply made her stand tall. Actually, she measured only five feet five inches in height. In her middle years, her short, stocky figure put on considerable weight, but the superb dignity and poise, the expressive eyes and the warm smile made her not only impressive but at times almost beautiful.

Recalling the early days when Mary on occasion spent time with the Luhans in Taos, Mabel wrote that

she was one of the best companions in the world in a house or on a trip. She loved to put on a big apron and go into our big old kitchen and toss a couple of pumpkin pies together. She loved to hob-nob, to sit and spin out reasons for strange happenings, to hear and tell about all the daily occurrences in both our lives. She was a romantic and loved the romance of the mystical and the occult and often induced in herself peculiar symptoms. She could see and hear and truly experience more than the rest of us, so when she least knew it she really became fascinatingly delphic and sibylline."[1]

## II  *The D. H. Lawrences*

The D. H. Lawrences arrived in Taos in 1923, the same year Mary Austin was deliberating between Santa Fe and Taos as a permanent home. As house guests of Mrs. Luhan on one occasion, Lawrence began to write a play about the company present, omitting his wife and himself. He entitled the drama *Altitude*. To begin the action, he imagined that the cook had not arrived to prepare breakfast. According to an editorial note prepared by one of the members of the cast at a later date, only one act was ever completed; and those lines were first set down on the back of a candy box one evening in Mrs. Luhan's living room. Several friends were present to offer suggestions as to what the characters should do and say. Everyone's general enthusiasm for being where he was under the circumstances is caught by Lawrence's dialogue. The satirical thrusts of Lawrence are typical and topical. However merited, they deserve to be discounted because of his humorous and somewhat vindictive intent.

The opening lines are delivered by Mary Austin as the curtain rises revealing the kitchen. She is standing in the sunny doorway chanting the invocation of a muezzin in a minaret, "Om," resoundingly, and turns to address the empty room: "This country is waiting. It lies spell-bound, waiting. The great South-west, America of America. It is waiting.... What for? What for?" The second character enters with his mind on breakfast, and asks "Hasn't the cook come?" Mary answers, "No sign of her yet." Then she questions the guest: "Isn't morning wonderful, here at this altitude, in the great South-West? Does it kindle no heroic response in you, young Intellectual?" The young intellectual, still mindful of his breakfast, replies: "I don't know. Maybe I'd better kindle a fire in the stove." "Quite right," Mary responds. "Homage to the god of fire. Wait! An apron! Let me do it. The fire in this house is the woman's fire. The fire in the camp is the man's fire. You know the Indians say that?" "No, I didn't know it till you told me," the young man admits. "Oh, young Intellectual," Mary scolds. "It is a Woman Mediator you are pining for. The Woman Redeemer."[2]

Before Act I of *Altitude* is finished, Mary Austin has cooked breakfast, but not until she has driven Mabel from the stove and informed her that she, Mary, is "officiating at this altar." Mabel has made a point that Joe, who has just brought in the water, has *life*, whereas the Anglos have only *nerves*: "The Indians are like glowing coals, and the white people are like ashes." Mary agrees that the Indians have something the white people need, a special rhythm, and that maybe in Taos the rhythm is at its height. The New York actress, one of the house guests, speaks one of her few lines when she asks, "You mean altitude?" and Mary explains, "The perfect rhythm of the American earth. The Indians have had it so long, maybe they're in danger of losing it." She plans to remain in Taos long enough to capture the revelation.

Lawrence has had fun in his tentative sketch of a play. As an Englishman and as a prophetic type himself, he would not adopt the gospel of salvation from any one else, though he sought human revelation in deed and word throughout the globe: Italy, Corsica, India, Australia, New Mexico, Mexico. Whether or not the utterance of a landscape could be translated so specifically as Mary Austin claimed, Lawrence was stimulated by the outer world almost as strongly as she was. He once wrote: "I think New Mexico was the greatest experience from the outside world that I have ever had. It certainly changed me forever. Curious as it may sound, it was New Mexico that liberated me from the present era of civilization, the great era of material and mechanical development."[3] As for the effect of the Indian dances upon D. H. Lawrence, both their glow and their rhythm can be felt in the New Mexico sketches found in his volume misnamed *Mornings in Mexico*. "The Dance of the Sprouting Corn" and "The Hopi Snake Dance" were never celebrated south of the American border.[4] After Lawrence returned to Europe, he longed for the restoration he had once felt in the air and sunshine he had jested about on the high plateau at Taos.

## III  *Life in Santa Fe*

Mary Austin chose Santa Fe for her permanent residence. After weeks in which she would be uncommunicative and isolated with her writing, the neighbors would be surprised to see her appear with a box of red raspberries, picked from her own garden. Mrs. Gerald Cassidy, one of these friends, describes the writing habits which reflect the absorption with which she concentrated on her work. Mrs. Cassidy met Mary in 1916 at a suffrage meeting in Atlantic City. They became friends and met again in New York City, where the Cassidys had leased a studio. While their studio was being prepared, Mrs. Austin invited them to be her guests at the National Arts Club. The day following their arrival at the club, Mary asked Ina Cassidy to come for tea to meet some of her fellow members. She exhibited every feeling of warmth and cordiality, but during the next two days they did not meet again. On the following morning, Mrs. Cassidy met Mary in the lobby and greeted her with a cheery "good morning." Mary Austin looked her straight in the face and apparently neither heard nor saw her. Mrs. Cassidy was stunned. She wondered how she could have offended the woman to such an extent. Two more days passed. On the third day, Mary called and in the most cordial tone, invited Mrs. Cassidy to breakfast. When they met there was no sign of any displeasure on Mrs. Austin's part and no mention was made of the encounter in the lobby. However, as they finished, Mary said, "Oh, I wanted to say, please don't pay any attention to my actions when you meet me in the morning. I may not see you or speak to you. But it is because I am deep in my work, and when I am I never allow anyone to speak to me. It breaks up the whole day for me, if I do. Please remember this and don't mind me. I wanted you to understand."[5]

In New Mexico, as in other parts of the United States, the folkways were changing. Tourists were flocking to the Indian pueblos to buy the pottery and jewelry in such quantities that the Indians could not fill the demand. Commercial dealers took Indians to Santa Fe and Albuquerque and provided them with machines so that they could turn out the rings and bracelets in quicker time and in greater numbers. The Navajo Indians were encouraged by traders to buy commercial dyes for their blankets and to simplify their designs. Young Indian boys in the government schools were trying to paint like the Anglo-American artists in Santa Fe, giving up the stylized figures of birds and animals in the symbolic two-dimensional world known to their pottery making and blanket weaving. Mary Austin became a leader in movements to stop these trends by helping to organize the Indian Arts Fund and by leaving the major portion of her estate to it at the time of her death. The fund was incorporated in 1925, and in 1928 it became affiliated with the Laboratory of Anthropology of Santa Fe, which today houses a collection second to none of Indian pottery, jewelry, and weaving. Research into the origins of Indian designs and craft technique is made possible through the fund.

The Spanish colonial crafts, too, were disappearing in New Mexico. The *artesanos* who had produced the carved chests, the hammered tin, the weaving, and the decorative embroidery were losing their market to the factory-produced objects which everywhere standardized American households. Mary Austin and Frank Applegate, an artist and writer whose knowledge of the Spanish crafts exceeded hers, joined forces to found the Spanish Colonial Arts Society, with the intention of preserving the best specimens of these folk arts and of reviving their practice. The Applegates, Frank and Alta, were neighbors, having built a large adobe house near the Camino del Monte Sol, which they furnished with the best of the Spanish handcrafts, the most skilled of which was the art of the *santero* or image maker. In the absence of religious art studios, the early Catholic churches of New Mexico had been equipped with figures of the saints carved *en bulto* and *en retablo*—"in form" and "in tablet or on flat board." Hundreds of these hand wrought statues and paintings were collected and preserved after they had been discarded from the modern church buildings. They were considered inappropriate to contemporary taste and worship.

Shortly after the New Mexico Folklore Society was founded in the spring of 1931, Mrs. Austin was invited to speak on the traditions of the Spanish Colonial Arts. In a hall facing on the Plaza of Old Town, Albuquerque, surrounded by the antique objects relating to her lecture, a Spanish shawl covering her shoulders and a black mantilla draping the high tortoise shell comb in her hair, Mary Austin talked of the isolation of New

Mexico as a province of Spain; the reliance placed upon the people to create for themselves the articles they needed; the response such necessity brought; the annual *conducta* or caravan to Chihuahua which established contact with Mexico and, through Mexico, with Spain.

## IV  *The Second Colorado River Conference*

This Mrs. Austin is scarcely the figure which might be expected to appear as a delegate to the Seven States Conference on water resources and the Colorado River. In 1927, the governor of New Mexico appointed her as one of the state's representatives to the Second Colorado River Conference, which began in Denver on August 22. The First Conference had met in Santa Fe in 1922, when Herbert Hoover was Secretary of the Interior. Mrs. Austin called these meetings some of the most representative conferences held since the Continental Congress in 1774, for there were delegates from political units covering a vast area of land and they were making decisions important for the welfare of many people for many generations. California and Arizona were concerned about the future of the Lower Basin of the Colorado; Nevada, Utah, Colorado, Wyoming, and New Mexico were involved in the life of the Upper Basin. Most of the water in the river came from the Upper Basin. Most of the population depending upon the supply of water for irrigation and power lived in the Lower Basin.

Here the claims of California and Arizona were a repetition of the argument twenty years earlier between Los Angeles and the Owens River, and the issues were the same. Did the demands of a larger population and industrial development outweigh the rights and privileges of a less populous area with equal potentials? In this battle, however, Arizona had stronger allies than the Owens Valley towns could find. Mary Austin fought for Arizona as she fought for Owens Valley. Making her voice heard in a number of the national as well as the regional publications, she pointed out that California contributed none of the water to the river, yet wanted to appropriate most of its flow. With her gift for analysis and expression, she wrote that "In Southern California boosting has become a religious duty; and the divine right of that section to all it can get, by any method whatever, is unquestioned."[7]

The dispute between the Southwestern states was something more than a fight for economic survival. She saw in it the national implications that lay in a land and its peoples to self-expression in terms of climate, topography, mineral wealth, and agricultural possibilities. The middle and the southern Rocky Mountain States with their great basins, pasture lands, mesas, and canyons offered the beginnings of a strongly marked culture. She opposed the rape of the natural resources of one state for the advantage of another. She also emphasized the international factors involved, since the Colorado River Waters were used below the Mexican border as well as above it.[8] Mrs. Austin did not live to see the issues settled, but the swing of the Upper Basin States to the side of Arizona in its David and Goliath struggle with California was eventually in line with her own point of view.

## V *Trip to Mexico*

She had started to go to Mexico in 1918. Having moved to New Mexico, she felt a greater need than ever to follow the stream of Spanish life to its sources. Mary Austin never traveled to Spain. She might well have done so when she was in Italy in 1908, but the pull of the Spanish tradition was not so strong at that time as it later became. Perhaps the folk movements of the American continents interested her more than similar expressions in Europe. She tried, in fact, to make the Indian folklore of America as vital and as interesting to readers as the folk tales of the Grimm brothers or those of Hans Christian Andersen. In Mexico the European genius and the Indian creative forces had merged. Dance dramas like the *matachines* performed in the Yaqui country of northern Mexico and in the villages, both Indian and Spanish, of Arizona and New Mexico combined the formations of ancient Moorish dances with those of Indian religious ritual. In 1931, she went to Mexico to lecture at the American Seminar sponsored by the Ministry of Education. The experience was memorable.

Before the murals of Diego Rivera, her imagination re-created the entire life of the American continent, seeing the patterns of early peoples emerging even in the braiding of women's hair and the movements of their bodies. Color, emotion, compassion, gratitude—all were woven into designs of beauty and harmony, and this was her vision of community life, whether then or now. Mary Austin dreamed her past into the present and planned a future from the best elements in both. She called these communal efforts the "American Rhythm," a term as mystical and yet as practical as her "Landscape Line." The murals of Rivera left her in tears,[9] for they portrayed the search for tenderness as well as strength. She shows no awareness that Rivera was identifying communality in early Aztec life with Marxian communism of today or the Indian tribal patterns with something quite similar to the patterns of socialized life recommended by Lenin.

Upon her return to New Mexico, Mrs. Austin compared the Mexican with the New Mexican world and found that the settlement of New Mexico had been less violent than the settlement of Mexico; that Indians had been enslaved in both places and intermarriage had occurred; that the great landed families preserved the social customs known in Spain; and that the peon class was satisfied with very little (most of which they could make for themselves) and enjoyed a communality of pleasures, such as fiestas, group sporting events, and religious ceremonials. At the time of the American occupation a good many of the Spanish natives were "fleeced" of their land and possessions because of unfamiliarity with Anglo-American business and legal practices. Subsequent to the introduction of commercial products from American factories, the native handcrafts disappeared. Through the encouragement of artists, writers, and enlightened educators in New Mexico, some of the native crafts could be revived. At Santa Fe an Indian Fair and a Spanish Market have provided an outlet for crafts of high quality, workmanship, and beauty.[10] If Mary Austin were living today, she would heartily approve of the annual New Mexico Arts and Crafts Fair held every August in the Old Town Plaza of Albuquerque. More than one hundred thousand people, including many tourists, patronize the numerous exhibitors whose booths display and sell the work of Indian, Spanish, and Anglo artisans.

## VI   *The San Jose Project*

In 1930 the New Mexico State Board of Education and the General Education Board of the Rockefeller Foundation joined with the University of New Mexico in sponsoring an experimental program in bilingual instruction among the rural population of the state. A pilot plan was inaugurated at the San Jose Training School in a largely Spanish district of Albuquerque. Mary Austin was a member of the Board of Directors. She held strong views on the nature of the project. Woodwork, weaving, tanning, tin-work, all the craft skills, were brought into the curriculum. The teaching of both English and Spanish was introduced at the lower grades, something never previously considered. Thus an attempt was made to offer competitive fields for both Anglo and Spanish children, in which the advantages and disadvantages of either group were more or less equalized and in which prestige barriers could be broken down. Mrs. Austin believed that the native Spanish children were not lower in intelligence than the Anglo children but were merely handicapped by the language factor and also by their environment. Almost no verbal testing could be devised which did not depend upon experience with the objects named and identified. The rural Spanish-speaking students of New Mexico lived in more primitive circumstances, read few if any books in English, but knew the names of animals in the fields and words for the native plants and farm tools used in agriculture. Such a background was a handicap to a Reading Test based upon the dominant urban environment of modern school children.

The San Jose Project terminated after five years, but it demonstrated that at an early age the gap between the Spanish-speaking and the English-speaking groups was not marked, but that, as the children grew older, the gap widened. The child learned from the sum total of his experience, and the Spanish children were exposed to an English-speaking environment only part of the day; the rest of the time the influence was Spanish. The *mores* of a Spanish-speaking community change slowly. The testing programs did not prove that the Spanish boys and girls were mentally less alert than the Anglo, only that they were poorly oriented in Anglo-American culture.[11] To a broader degree, so were the Indian young people, once placed in the standard educational program of the United States Government School. When asked to draw a cow or a deer, instead of just identifying one, an Indian boy ordinarily did a better job than the Anglo. The testing depended upon the type of acquaintance demanded: verbal memory, eye recognition, or first-hand experience.

Mary Austin insisted that the standard program in public schools did not provide sufficient avenues for creative expression upon the part of the alien groups in the United States. "Alien" seems a peculiar term for Indians who anticipated the colonizers from the Spanish peninsula by several thousand years. Nor does the term fit the Spanish Europeans who preceded the English on American soil by several decades. It was to accommodate the vague term "education" to these separately oriented and non-English groups that Mary Austin sought to bend the curriculum and school activities in ways expansive and instructive to all the groups. Her point of view found support and has been realized in the more flexible program adopted, stressing Indian, Spanish, and Anglo in the language, vocational, and recreational fields.

On June 5, 1933, the University of New Mexico conferred upon Mary Austin the degree of Honorary Doctor of Letters. Departing from academic custom, she was asked to speak to the graduating class for a few moments at the close of the ceremonies. Her words were to the effect that study was a challenge extending beyond diploma days: "I have always been a learner. If the honors which come to me are in any way deserved, it is because through my life I have gone on learning. I do not intend to leave off the process even with death."

At the dinner held in her honor following the commencement, she told the story of the army officer whose uniform was decorated with an array of many shining medals. When someone asked how he had won so many awards, he pointed to the smallest of the medals and said, "I won this for a little skirmish in the first battle I ever engaged in, and then"—pointing to the next medal, which was larger and brighter—"I won this because I'd won the first."—and so on. The point she made was that anyone's career began with taking a stand for the things he believed in. His achievement came as he followed through, fighting for the people and causes he thought worth while.

She illustrated her story about the medals by briefly mentioning some of the worthy battles she had fought in her lifetime and what she meant to accomplish in the next thirty years!

A week afterwards, Mrs. Frank Applegate, a neighbor of Mary Austin on the Camino, invited a few Santa Fe and Albuquerque people to have tea with "Dr. Mary." Among those attending was John Crowe Ransome, of Kenyon College, distinguished as poet and critic, who had been teaching that summer at the University of New Mexico, and who emphasized the major importance of esthetic criteria over historical, biographical, and linguistic data for understanding individual literary works of art. B. A. Botkin and his wife also were guests. Botkin, then at the University of Oklahoma, had published an anthology of regional verse, *Southwest Scene,* and was later to edit such volumes as *Folk-Say,* and collections of American folklore. Philip Stevenson, a playwright, and some others were also present. At the tea "Dr. Mary" talked about primitive drama. She had lectured on Folk Theater at the University of California and at the Yale Department of Drama. In New Haven, she had produced a version of the "Guadalupe Play," portraying the story of the Mexican peon, Juan Diego, who reported his conversation with the Virgin Mary on a hill called Tepeyacac in 1531. Despite some skepticism on the part of the Yale Drama School staff, the play was a success; and Mary Austin intended, had she lived, to make a survey of such folk plays, secular as well as religious, and to promote their translation and revival.[12] As she talked on this occasion, she mentioned having been ill. The signs showed in the greyness of her face and in the slight sag of her figure, which had always been strong in posture.

During the decade Mary Austin lived in Santa Fe, she saw the publication of eight new books and the re-publication of two older ones. The new works were *The American Rhythm, The Land of Journeys' Ending, The Children Sing in the Far West, Starry Adventure, Experiences Facing Death, Earth Horizon, One-Smoke Stories,* and *Can Prayer be Answered.* The two reprints were *Lands of the Sun* and *The Man Jesus.* Only one of these books was a novel, *Starry Adventure.* Herein may be read the story of her writing career, a story to be examined in greater detail during the chapters to follow in this book. The writing by Mary Austin which most holds the attention and is sought as a well of refreshment is her story of places, of the elemental experiences of people finding out about them, and of their living upon the primary resources they provide. From her point of view, the experiences of a prospector in the Kearsarge Canyons or of a vineyardist in the Cerro Gordo are not the impoverished lessons of survival; they convey most of the fundamental truths of human learning, truths to be considered as antidotes to the lessons provided in industrial slums where minds are torn and bodies worn.

## VII   Earth Horizon

On December 5, 1932, a large group of Mrs. Austin's friends gathered at the Applegate home to congratulate Mary upon the publication of *Earth Horizon,* her autobiography. The large living room of the Spanish colonial house was filled with smoke. Thin shafts of light fell from tin light-fixtures fastened to the dark beams, and the flames from piñón logs danced shadows on the white walls. Mary Austin sat in a high-backed wicker-woven chair. In a pleasant, calm voice, sometimes hesitating but always on its way to a clear statement, she reviewed her experiences as a writer:

> From the time I was thirteen there has been nothing new in my life. What I should do later on was pretty clear to me then. I realized that I should be interested in people, for I was then. I liked the place I lived in and the people with whom I lived, though there was nothing dramatic about my life, and no contacts which could be called literary.
>
> What I did in the way of study of people in cities, of the Indians in their villages, of literary folk in art communities has been directed by some design in my life for which I am not responsible. I knew when I was very young that I should have a good deal of mystical experience, but I have always felt that I was not doing it, that something outside me was responsible, that I was not the shaper but the shaped.[13]

Mary Austin was often accused of cultivating an enormous ego. Yet in her talk she denied her own individuality in creating books; she attributed them to something greater than herself. When another writer once complained of a lack of self-confidence, Mary snapped: "That's the most conceited remark I've ever heard anyone make. . . . You are assuming that you yourself do the writing. It is the All-Knowing Intelligence that writes through you. When *you* say you lack confidence and you do the writing, you're putting yourself on a plane with God."[14]

At the Applegate house that night her audience was absorbed to hear her confess that she had been lonesome most of her life, that she was sustained by her sense of mission, that she felt an unconscious direction of her creative energies. "I knew that I had lived symbolically, that I had done what any woman perhaps could have done, but which for some reason or other most of them do not do. I was the medium, the tool of forces I could not control."

The poet and translator Witter Bynner, author of *The Beloved Stranger, Indian Earth, Eden Tree* and *The Jade Mountain,* asked, "Didn't you want anyone to share your work with you?" "Yes, I did," Mary Austin answered, "but I never found anyone. There were two or three men with whom I was congenial; two of them I became engaged to marry. But when we went places, they usually came home mad. Either I had received more attention than they did, or I'd had to tell them to shut up and let me talk. They came away mad. I know that many people are disappointed that I didn't write more of my sex life, but all that was important to me I wrote about it. None of my affairs of the heart ever made any difference to me, to what I had to say." There were some murmurs of dissent in the crowd, and Mary laughed: "I'm writing a book now on the subject. The title may be *Love Is Not Enough.*"

During the summer of 1933 Mary Austin attended a conference on Regional Literature at the University of Montana in Missoula. "Art," she said, "considered as the expression of any people as a whole, is the response they make in various mediums to the impact that the totality of their experiences makes upon them, and there is no sort of experience that works so constantly and subtly upon man as his regional environment."[15] She pointed to the contrasting cultures of Classic Greece and ancient Egypt; to the distinctions between Scotch, Irish, and British literature, still not erased by long association under one political identity; to the Moorish and Iberian elements in Spanish art. There is not one standardized America, though Europeans seized upon

*Babbit* as such a portrait. Mrs. Austin called Sinclair Lewis' creation "the broad, thin, generalized surface reflection" of an American type, one that has risen out of a "footless" way of life that is widely shared in communities of the United States. That *Babbit* represents the deepest and rooted types of American activity, she denied.

For her choices of the rooted type she nominated Hawthorne's *The House of the Seven Gables,* unmistakably stamped by New England; Henry James's *Washington Square,* with the same imprint of provincial New York; Mark Twain's *Tom Sawyer* and *Huckleberry Finn,* indelibly marked by the Mississippi Valley; and Willa Cather's *My Antonia,* stamped as pioneer Nebraska. She might have nominated Adolph Bandelier's *The Delight Makers* as a novel which could have been written only in the Pueblo Country of the American Southwest. The literary habit since Mary Austin made her address has been to decry the regional note as somehow limited in esthetic scope. At the University of Montana Conference, a member of the English Department challenged Mrs. Austin with the question, "Would you say that Milton in writing *Paradise Lost* was creating a regional poem?" She thought a moment and then answered, "I would say it was regional in time."

"Doctor Mary" was the despair of her medical doctor. She refused to observe directions about her diet as to either quality or quantity, and she gave her overtaxed heart little rest. Shortly before she died, she expressed a desire to attend the Fiesta of San Isidro in a little village to the west of Santa Fe. A friend took her there; and, as the car drew up to the church, the people were carrying the little wooden image of the saint out of the church to march with it in procession through the fields. As Mary watched she said, "I think I'd like to follow them, too." She slipped out of the car, and started after San Isidro as he blessed the fields. She went only a few yards before her friend had to help her back into the car.[16]

## VIII   *Poets' Roundup*

Only her indomitable will power enabled her to take part in the Poets' Roundup, an afternoon of readings inaugurated by Alice Corbin Henderson, one of the co-sponsors, with Harriet

Monroe, in founding *Poetry Magazine* in 1912. Mrs. Henderson had been living in Chicago, where she knew Carl Sandburg, Vachel Lindsay, and others who helped to make *Poetry* one of the leading mediums for expression in the English-speaking world. After a breakdown in health in 1916, she had moved to Santa Fe. While recovering from the threat of tuberculosis which kept her in the sanitarium for a year, she built a house on the Camino del Monte Sol and became one of those who established studios which later made the road famous. Her husband, William Penhallow Henderson, was an architect as well as an artist. In 1925 the Santa Fe poets began to meet at the Henderson home one evening a week for fellowship and the reading of their poems. Five years later, this group and others sought a way to raise money for the Southwest Indian Association. Alice Corbin proposed public readings by the local poets and someone suggested that the poets wear Western costumes. "Then it can be a rodeo" another suggested, "or a round-up of poets."[17]

On August 9, 1934, the roundup included, among the fifteen readers, John Gould Fletcher, Witter Bynner, Alice Corbin Henderson, Dorothy Belle Hughes, Langdon Mitchell, Haniel Long, Stanley Vestal, and Mary Austin. Mrs. Austin's name did not appear on the Master-of-Ceremonies' typewritten list. Mary had not been well enough to attend the rehearsal on the evening before, and no one expected her to show up. But, as the readings began, Mary Austin appeared at the home where the program was being held. She walked out upon the terrace of the garden and was introduced to the audience as "for years the boss of the crowd." She wore a dark silk dress with a lace scarf thrown over her shoulders. Her face was very pale, but she read her poems with a firm voice, the deep quality vibrant and rich. But the shadow was there. Five days later, she died.[18]

Death came as she slept in the afternoon. Mary Austin once wrote to a friend that death seemed like a ship sailing on the stream of consciousness, until it began to sink, deeper and deeper, finally disappearing from the time element.[19] She believed that there was an immortal quality in the psyche of man; that subjective consciousness became part of all the living essence in nature; that it was a separate stream from the physical elements that are continually re-created in natural substance. God, she called "the experiencable quality in the universe," and she once wrote of Jesus as the man who reached the highest union in this spiritual state.[20]

At the Poets' Roundup, she had read a poem called "In Papagueria" along with four short poems called "Prayers to the Outdoor Saints." All were taken from her book *The Children Sing in the Far West*. The "Outdoor Saints" were: Saint Doucelina, "whose eyes did see the peach turn rosy on the tree"; San Isidro, the farmers' saint, whom she asked to plough for her as the angels once for him held "the furrow true"; Our Lady of Guadalupe, whom she prayed to smile on her garden as she did upon the bare rocks which made "roses bloom" for the Mexican peasant Juan Diego; and finally San Francisco, who "Walked in the wilderness, Preaching to wolf and snake Kindness for Jesus sake."[21] Now her form lay quiet at the front of her living room in "The Beloved House" while the pastor of an Episcopal Church read prayers in a language unfamiliar to her saints. Iron-branched candelabra held tapers that shed a warm light upon the familiar Spanish shawl and the tall comb, a *peineta*, set in her hair.

Following the ritual of the minister, two poems were read which Mary Austin had composed in anticipation of her death. In each of them she asks to be buried in the mountains, in such a place as she had known and appreciated in her books of nature. The first poem is reproduced here. The second is printed in Chapter 8, which treats of her poetry.

## GOING WEST

Some day I shall go West,
Having won all time to live it in, at last
Too still to boast.
But when I smell the sage,
When the long, marching landscape line
Melts into wreathing mountains,
And the dust cones dance
Something in me that is of them shall stir.

Happy, if I come home
When the musk-scented, moon-white gilia blows,
When all the hills are blue, remembering
The sea from which they rose.
Happy again
When blunt-faced bees carouse
In red flagons of the incense shrub
Or apricots have lacquered boughs,
And trails are dim with rain.

Lay me where some contented oak can prove
How much of me is nurture for a tree;
Sage thoughts of mine
Be acorn clusters for the deer to browse.
My moving whimsies—will you chide again
When they come up as lantern flowers?

I shall be small and happy as the grass,
Proud if my tip
Stays white, webby moons the spider weaves,
Or down my bleaching stalks shall slip
The light, imprisoning dew,
Where once you trod
I shall be bluets in the April sod.

Or if the wheel should run too fast,
Run up and rest
As a sequoia for a thousand years.[21]

There was no music, and at the close of the prayers and the reading of the poems, the casket was closed and carried out to the Camino. The hearse and the cars following it rolled down the then unimproved road, through the city, and past the capitol to the Fairview Cemetery where a temporary interment was made in the family vault of a prominent Santa Fe family. This course of action was taken to allow time for a deliberate choice of a final resting place. After two years of indecision by the trustees of Mrs. Austin's estate, the body was removed from the vault and cremated; the ashes were then held by a Santa Fe mortuary for a year. Discussion of her burial was not limited to the trustees. Ernest Thompson Seton, widely known author and founder of Seton Village five miles east of

Santa Fe, offered a site for her grave on one of the hills near his community. There was even talk of interment on the grounds of Casa Querida, her home.

## IX  *Mt. Picacho: Summit Top*

Although she had left no statement in her will, Mary Austin had discussed her final resting place with a number of her friends. One of them was a forest ranger named Dave Steele. He had fenced the United States Park Service lands up to the summit of the mountain peak directly east of Mary Austin's home. It is a pointed eminence, very symmetrical. The name is Picacho, which means "summit top" in Spanish. Here the trustees finally decided to place the ashes of the woman whom Carl Van Doren called "Master of the American Environment" whose books were "wells driven into America to bring up water for her countrymen though they might not have realized their thirst."[23]

On Wednesday, August 13, 1937, four saddle horses and a pack horse formed a procession through the streets of Santa Fe and headed for Mt. Picacho. The riders were Dave Steele, his son, a nephew, and Ray Otis, a Santa Fe novelist and long-time friend of Mrs. Austin. The pack horse carried cement, sand, and water to seal Mary Austin's ashes into the rock at an unmarked spot located at the peak. The ride took the travelers up the Camino and past her house to a trail at the south end of the mountain. Up through the trees and over the strewn boulders and pine needles the caravan moved. Below the ridge, the valley spread for miles to the distant ramparts of the Jemez peaks. Overhead, the dome of blue poured out and upward into a boundless horizon. Stopping at a fence, the riders dismounted, tied the horses, and carried the saddle bags to a cairn of rocks not far from the summit. There the ashes were sealed in a crevice; and, while Steele tossed the metal container over the crest into a canyon, Otis used a stick to write the name "Mary Austin" in the cement. Steele tried to erase it, but the cement had partially set and the letters remained.[24]

Today only traces of the name can be read, but the legacy of Mary Austin's books has not been effaced by the passing of the years. In fact, they are beginning to reappear in paperback editions. Collections of her periodical essays and short stories, hitherto unavailable in book form, are scheduled for re-publication. In 1915, H. G. Wells predicted that the work of Mary Austin would live "when many of the more portentous reputations of today may have served their purpose in the world and become no more than fading names."[25] This prediction seems more than likely to come true.

# PART II: THE NOVELIST

No one in America writes a better novel than Mary Austin, . . .
When the story of the American novel has been told fifty years
from now, Mary Austin's name will stand well up among the
major novelists of the new century.

—WILLIAM ALLEN WHITE

For she can do, has done, what no other American writer could
accomplish. Whenever she tries to do the regulation thing, in a
conventional form, she does it rather badly; at best, indifferently.
The trouble is, she has genius of much too large a denomination
to be available for current use; she has to convert it, at a constant loss, into the talents of ordinary circulation.

—GRANT OVERTON

## CHAPTER 5

# Social Protest

THE NOVEL, as a literary type, was originally a short story. Both the French *novelle* and the Italian *novella* are diminutives of words meaning "new" and "strange," something a reader has not heard before. Both are related to the English word *news*, and invite the interest of readers upon the basis of stories traveling the rounds because they are arresting and informative. With the development of Medieval European tales into long prose narratives, involving sizable groups of characters and episodes linked to cover entire lifetimes or even epochs, novels became social documents of wide proportions, frequently presenting interpretations of an entire society or of nations from the author's point of view.

## I "The Novel of Tomorrow"

The role of fiction was discussed in a symposium called "The Novel of Tomorrow," conducted by the *New Republic* magazine in 1922. Two contrasting attitudes were expressed by Willa Cather and Mary Austin in their contributions. In 1920, Mrs. Austin had written *No. 26 Jayne Street*, which she felt was her finest effort in fiction. Miss Cather in 1922 was to publish *One of Ours*, and she wrote: "If the novel is a form of imaginative art, it cannot be at the same time a vivid and brilliant form of journalism.... How wonderful it would be if we could throw all the furniture out of the window; and along with it, all the tiresome old patterns, and leave the room as bare as the stage of a Greek theatre; or as the house into which the Glory of Pentecost descended; leave the scene bare for the play of emotions, great and little—for the nursery tale, no less than the tragedy, is killed by tasteless amplitude. The elder Dumas enunciated a great principle when he said that to make a drama a man needed one passion and four walls."[1]

Mrs. Austin wrote that in her opinion the novel had always been preoccupied with the meaning of its own age, and the novelist must choose whether to concentrate upon the individual pattern or upon the social pattern. She remarks upon the changing design of American society and asserts that the novelist must get inside this design:

> The democratic novelist must be inside his novel rather than outside in the Victorian fashion of Thackeray or the reforming fashion of Mr. Wells. He may, like Mr. Sherwood Anderson, be so completely inside as to be unclear in his conclusion about the goal, but there he is, Americanly, on his way. The reference of personal conduct to an overhead Judgment which forced the earlier novelist to assume the God in the disposition of his characters, has here given place to a true democratic desire of man to see himself as he is seen by the people with whom he does business. His search is not so much for judgment as for revelation, quick, nervous appreciations of place, relationship and solidarity. But in every case the validity of the American form will rest upon that intuitive access to the collective consciousness, which it is the dream, and probably the mission of democracy to achieve.[2]

In the opinion of Mary Austin, a novel becomes a social document, a transcript of the society which produces it; but, at the same time, its author reveals awareness of the best or worst directions in which that society is traveling. Miss Cather shows her absorption in the personal portrait, a success which many believe she achieved more notably with *My Antonia*, produced in 1915, than she did with *One of Ours* in 1922. The latter novel, which assayed social appraisal, shifted its scene from the locale of Nebraska to the battlefields of Europe, and perhaps thereby departed farther from the ideal she found in the single passion within four walls.

In discussing the work of Mrs. Austin as a novelist in the succeeding three chapters, I shall not attempt to follow chronology. Rather, I shall consider her nine novels in terms of their common motivating impulses: social protest, feminism, and the romantic approach to living. Although protest was innate in her, the success in voicing it through her books *The Ford* and *No. 26 Jayne Street* met with only limited public approval. Her stand as a feminist in *A Woman of Genius* found a wider appeal. She tried to extend this public image in *Love and the Soul Maker.* All of her books assessing the social awareness of Americans to romance, from the way of life portrayed in *Isidro* to the expression in *Starry Adventure,* seemed to be weighted less heavily with "collective consciousness" and to succeed, therefore, better as stories. From the chronological point of view, Mrs. Austin began writing in the romantic vein and ended there. First, however, we must inquire into her probing the "collective mind" in the middle period of her novel writing.

## II  The Ford

*The Ford,* published in 1917, is created from the author's life experiences at Tejon Pass and at Bishop, California, with some echo of those in the New Theater in New York City. The plot centers around the family of a rancher named Steven Brent who lives at Las Palomitas in southern California. Brent and his neighbors own oil properties, and they also hope for water from an irrigation project in the valley of Tierra Longa. The valley is a thinly disguised version of the Owens River terrain where the Austins lived from 1892 to 1906. The Brents have a son Kenneth and a daughter Anne. The daughter is a projection of the author herself, as both she and her heroine fought to save a region from predatory outside interests. A good deal of symbolism emerges as the story unfolds.

At the outset of the plot, a group of children, playing on the bank of a stream, are acting out the episode in the Bible where Jacob wrestles with the angel. Kenneth Brent is Jacob, and a neighbor girl, Virginia Grant, is the angel. In the Biblical account, the drama requires that the angel should triumph, but Kenneth grabs his adversary about the hips and tosses her down the bank. When the angel objects to this reversal of Scripture, Frank protests that the girls always play they are angels and the boys have to do the pretending. When Virginia claims that he tricked her, Kenneth offers to do it again. The stream of water beside which the children play becomes a symbol in the book for the need and proper use of water. The creek, out of control, nearly drowns a lamb and Kenneth, too, who has been herding the lamb.

The wrestling match is remembered years later when both Virginia and Kenneth are romantically involved. She has pursued a career in feminist causes in the East, having taken to lecturing against the abuses of the capitalistic system and in behalf of the labor movement, along with woman's emancipation through the ballot box and freedom through more liberal divorce laws. After an unhappy marriage, Virginia returns to California. In San Francisco, she acts the leading role in a play dealing with human rights; but, when Kenneth comes for a reunion with her, headlines reveal the scandal of her family life; her alienated former husband is accused of being the father of an illegitimate child. Brent also hears from the playwright that Virginia has been his mistress. The angel seems to have tossed herself down a bank without any help from Jacob.

The "ford" in the novel is not only a meeting place for farmers but a dividing line for the oil workers who are constructing a pipe line from the wells. After drilling brings in oil from various holdings, including those of Steven Brent, a powerful landowner named Rickart gains control of the line and closes it down to individual well diggers. The United States Reclamation Service makes surveys for a dam in the valley, and a real estate agent appears in Tierra Longa signing options for the valley land. His name is Elwood, a transparent reflection of Frederick Eaton, the Los Angeles mayor who turned land agent. When a government surveyor named Lattimore resigns to join the water district of a great city, the identification with William Mulholland of Los Angeles becomes crystal clear. However, the irrigation battle in *The Ford* is waged between the valley and San Francisco rather than with Los Angeles; and there is a happy ending to the story.

Anne Brent goes into real estate, and Kenneth Brent organizes the ranchers to oppose the Old Man Rickart. A division of the water is made between the city and the valley. Steve Brent recalls the years he and his wife fought to survive on their ranch at Las Palomitas. "Over there," he says, "from the top of San Anselmo, the Spanish padres blessed it ... where the town stands there was a roadhouse when Fremont forded the river. Fifty years ago, when my father drove over the Pass, there was this

house here, and the hacienda at Agua Caliente.... Water, water
and power ... and farms, not cities."[3] The message and symbolism are clear. Kenneth Brent, like the author, felt the claim of
the land. He saw his mother sacrificed to it, through disappointment and heartbreak. He helped his father triumph with the
land at Las Palomitas. Playing the role of the Biblical Jacob,
he learned that angels have their problems as well as men
and that some of them will not wait seven years for a husband.
He does marry, however, and happily when he falls in love
with the sister of the playwright. Anne Brent loses her childhood
sweetheart, Frank Rickart; but she earns both his devotion and
the respect of his father, the Old Man of the Valley.[4]

## III No. 26 Jayne Street

The second of Mrs. Austin's novels dealing with social institutions has less symbol and more protest. The locale for *No. 26
Jayne Street* is New York City; the settings are drawing rooms
in Greenwich Village, or along Fifth Avenue, and at the Brevoort
Hotel in the East Thirties. At No. 26 Jayne Street, the central
character, Neith Schuyler, has created a hideaway in order to
escape the domination of two aristocratic old aunts. She has
been living with them since the death of her father several years
ago. Now she wants to face the world by herself because she
has many decisions to make. The time is 1914, and the United
States is on the verge of war in Europe. A man named Adam
Frear has come into her life. She met him while traveling with
her father in Europe. He awakened in her thoughts of a new
social order. She heard him lecture upon the new freedom in
social attitudes. Mrs. Austin's names frequently give clues to
ideological intentions for the characters. "Adam" certainly means
the first, last, and always Male personality. "Frear" may be a
disguised "Freer"—free in his thinking and a liberator of the
mind. One of the characters in the book, a war correspondent
named Van Harwood, puns upon *Jayne Street* as "Jane Street,"
intimating that Neith has turned her home into a hall for
feminine crusaders.

Syndicalism, socialism, free love, women's suffrage, low wages,
poor housing, subsistence living, war, democracy, capitalism,
autocracy, Europe, America, art, the New York skyline, money,

poverty, social imagination—such words sprinkle the pages of *No. 26 Jayne Street*. They are spoken by Hippolyte Leninsky ("Son of Lenin"), a Russian Marxist and editor of *The Proletariat;* and also by Sadie Comyns ("the Common People"?), a Russian Jewess who teaches school in New Jersey; by Direck Kendries, an active organizer of labor, not just a lecturer (could his given name mean "Direct"?); by Fleta Spence, a social reconstructionist ("Flitter moth"?); and by the radical journalist Van Harwood ("Hard Wood"?), and others.

Adam Frear wins the love of Neith Schuyler, who is drawn to his crusade; for she discerns the indifference of her wealthy and socially conscious family and their friends. "This, then, was the American bond, to be bound for the same place, or at least in the same direction. Democracy, of course, could have nothing to do with the place from which you came. And Adam Frear's testing attitude had meant simply that he wished to make certain that she was worthy to march in the direction from which the light arose that illuminated him. It was the final note of her conclusion that he had been so patently pleased."[5]

The abstract concepts are illustrated by specific episodes, such as the strike at the Marcy Mills (largely owned by members of Neith Schuyler's family) and peace rallies by women's groups agitating against entering World War I. Eustace Rittenhouse, a suitor of Neith, joins the English Air Force and is eventually killed in Europe. To Neith, the great social movements in the world boil down to personal attitudes of individuals toward one another. She reads Adam Frear's books and articles with a curious feeling of unreality. An acquaintance of Mary Austin has identified Frear with Lincoln Steffens, whom she had known since the days at Carmel.[6] Steffens was two years older than Mary, and had combined editorial work on *McClure's* the *American Magazine*, and *Everybody's* with sensational newspaper articles on municipal corruption. During the period of *No. 26 Jayne Street* he was a leading figure in the American Radical movement. Mrs. Austin mentions him in her autobiography as one of the Carmel colony.[7] Whether the portrait is literal or not, Neith Schuyler begins to translate Adam Frear's wide political outlook into personal terms. Was he as generous in personal relationships as he was when he looked out upon society? Neith is still drawn to Lt. Rittenhouse, but she has not committed herself to either man.

When the Marxist Leninsky is found distributing pamphlets to workers in a war plant, he is beaten by New York police. He dies from the injuries. His common-law wife is expecting a baby. These events turn Neith away from capitalistic society and to an acceptance of Adam Frear, who has just ended a trip to Russia. He has brought back briefcases stuffed with notes for writing and lecturing. They postpone their wedding until he can catch up on his work. Some months of happy associations pass until on one occasion Adam and Neith are standing before a jeweler's window. Neith expresses her delight in what she sees, and Adam asks whether he may buy her something. The shopkeeper places a tray of rings and bracelets before them. Neith inquires whether Adam would think an engagement ring a bourgeois gesture. She is relieved to learn that he does not think so. They select tiny square-cut emeralds in an antique setting. Adam has been called to Washington for a meeting with the President. They agree to a quiet marriage upon his return.

Two days later Neith Schuyler has a visitor. A woman calls upon her and asks whether Adam has given her a letter. Neith learns that the letter was withheld. Discovering this, the woman reveals that she had previously been engaged to Adam Frear in much the same secluded way that he is now engaged to Neith. The woman is Rose Matlock (one wonders if a verbal cipher appears here as "mate-lock"?). She had been a teacher in a Western university when Frear came on a lecture tour. Their interest in each other developed several years later when she moved to New York. Rose has scarcely filled in this background before Adam Frear enters the room. The sight of her enrages him, and words and gestures are threatening: "What did I tell you if you *dared* to.... I deny that you are concerned in my affairs at all.... What do you want?"[8]

Perhaps this is neither the dialogue nor the episode from which contemporary novels build into best-sellers. What Mary Austin has done is to bring a social reformer into a situation requiring personal reformation. He has caught two fine women with the same bait: his personal charm and his idealism. The second woman, upon finding out that the first was discarded like a silk scarf, resents his attitude and joins the other woman against him. Rose still loves Adam, but he refuses to recognize that she has any rights to do so: "I deny that you are concerned in my affairs at all!"

The novel ends in the next twenty pages. Word comes to Neith that Lt. Rittenhouse, the young pilot who loved her, has gone down in his plane over France. His death brings reunion to the estranged parents, but no reunion comes to Adam and Neith. She judges him to be a fraud whose actions are centered as much upon personal gratification and selfish desires as were those of her own relatives toward the strikers or the city police in their treatment of Hippolyte Leninsky. She returns Adam's letters and ring, and then meets for a post-mortem with Rose Matlock. Rose reports that Adam has taken a ship for the Far East. The women agree that they have been rather too much for him. On the last page, Neith wonders whether he will ever come back. The reader concludes that he never will.

Mary Austin has left the problem unsolved. The reader who finishes the book will not solve it either. What does a man owe to a woman who still loves him? Or, reversing the situation, what does a woman owe a man who continues to love her after she has turned to someone else? Should each dispose of the matter as did Adam Frear? "I deny that you are concerned in my affairs at all."

CHAPTER *6*

# The Feminist

MARY AUSTIN'S CRUSADE for women's rights began as a child. In her autobiography she describes how she waged with her family the battle of the "four-minute egg." Scrambling out of sleep at an early hour and before her appetite was fully aroused, she was not prepared to face a very soft boiled egg. This was the way the others liked their eggs. Mary's father was dead, and now the head of the house was, to all appearances, brother Jim, two years her elder. She asked to have the egg kept in the kettle one minute longer, and even volunteered to look after the egg herself. Both requests struck the mother and brother as unreasonable. Why should she be different? Mary seems to have decided then that a home should be a democratic institution and not a little kingdom where the males were enthroned.

One of the minor characters in *No. 26 Jayne Street*, actress Madeline Sherrod, had remarked to Neith Schuyler that if she ever reached a position where she had to depend upon public appreciation she would discover "a wall of men, a felted, almost sound-proof wall of male intelligence, male reporters, critics, managers" that had to be breached or circumvented.[1] Olivia Lattimore, the actress of the earlier novel *A Woman of Genius*, discovers that her problems with men began, like the author's, as a child. In fact, Olivia is a projection of Mary in all respects except the two most important ones: Mary never followed the stage for a career, and she never made a career of living with men. Perhaps this is why the private life of Olivia Lattimore occupies three-quarters of the book, the social and professional life only one-quarter. The reader wonders which period of the life of a genius is the more important, the preliminary or the final stage, the growth or the fulfillment.

### I   Revolt from the Village: Olivia Lattimore

Edward Wagenknecht, chronicler of the American novel, points out that the "revolt from the village," which was to be proclaimed later in Sinclair Lewis' *Main Street*, was already implied in *A Woman of Genius*. Olivia Lattimore's story deals with "everything that is important in woman's rebellion against man, for on its deepest level the book is a study of creative power, of its connection with sexual power, of how it is differentiated from sexual power, and of the conflict between art and love."[2]

*A Woman of Genius* gets off to an incredibly bad start. Instead of beginning with the child prodigy (since she is a genius, and the reader is to learn about her youth), the storyteller, Olivia, spends five pages—all of Chapter One—explaining how she came to write about herself. She was compelled to write her autobiography to show other women the problems she had been through, and the chief woman she had in mind was Pauline Mills, a conventionally minded girl with whom she had grown up. However, Pauline's husband, doubtless, would read the book and censor it. Pauline, who usually listened to her husband, therefore might never see it at all.[3]

This opening has some merit, for it suggests that the novel may be forbidden fruit to the conventionally minded, a sure invitation to the reader to expect exciting developments. They do not arrive for the first half of the book; when they do, the story gains in interest. This change may be because the modern reader finds the author's background as trying as she did, but with less personal concern. Taylorville, in the fictitious state called Ohianna, where Olivia Lattimore spent her early days, is obviously Carlinville, Illinois. The town square, enclosed by a hitching rack and screened by maples, with the Methodist Church guarding one side and the courthouse the other, represents the heart of an environment typical in the Middle West. Untypical is the child Olivia, who creates an imaginary deity or spirit named Snockerty, to whom she chants incantations and makes offerings at a woodland altar. Snockerty, who lived in a hollow apple tree, was propitiated by rites consisting of Sunday School hymns, school recitations, mock prayers, and even anathemas picked up in some book of witch tales. They were adapted to immediate needs, such as scaring the neighbors' children and providing dramatic soliloquies of the highest eloquence.

Olivia's childhood is told much as Mary Austin retold her own story twenty years later when she wrote *Earth Horizon*, but in her autobiography Mrs. Austin substituted the facts for the pseudo-fictitious details in the novel. The part of *A Woman of Genius* for which the author could not supply the elements from her own life are those when Olivia Lattimore goes to Chicago and becomes an actress on the professional stage. She plays in a stock company; nearly starves when the season ends and her contract ceases. Finally, she meets a playwright and a producer who become steppingstones to her success. Her genius unfolds on the New York stage. There her ties to Gerald McDermott, the playwright, become stronger. He is married and has two children, but emotionally he has been drifting for years, chiefly to actresses and dancers. To avoid the entanglement with Gerald, Olivia goes to London. There at a reception given by wealthy Americans she encounters a man she had formerly met in Taylorville. He was the first man who had ever kissed her. Their meeting had been a dramatic one.

Years ago, when she was living in Taylorville, she had attended a picnic where a visiting youth had surprised her while she was reciting verses in the woods. He had applauded the performance from the vantage point of a rail fence and then introduced himself as the nephew of a prominent Taylorville farmer. He had been invited to the picnic, but his horse became lame and he had to walk the way to the lake shore. The stranger lived in Chicago, where he said he often went to the theater. As they walked back to the other young people, he grew more and more animated in his talk. When a gust of wind blew them closer together, he kissed her. The moment was an electric one, marred only because they were observed and a minor scandal developed among the gossips. Olivia's mother forbade her to see the boy again and returned the letter he wrote to Olivia without letting her know that it had come. Olivia married a hometown boy, Tommy Bettersworth, who had a job in a tailor shop. After a few years of unhappy marriage, they separated and were only reconciled at Tommy's deathbed.

In London, Olivia now met after so long a lapse of time the boy she had never forgotten. Nor had he forgotten her. In fact, they discovered they had always been in love, though each had been married; and, except for one occasion when they had seen each other at a political gathering in Chicago, they had not met nor spoken. Helmeth Garrett, the sweetheart of her youth, has become an engineer, thereby fulfilling the ambition he had talked of that summer day in Taylorville. She, too, has realized her ideal of becoming an actress, as she had dreamed in the woods. The crisis in Olivia Lattimore's life now is at hand. Was she to choose the Shining Destiny, the stuff from which she had built her dreams, with children growing up about her in the conventional social norm, or should she follow the Gift, which in one place she describes as a power descending from some high unknowable source "fluttering low like a dove, hovering over me."[4]

Olivia temporarily gives herself to Helmeth. When he wants her to marry him and go to Mexico where he has an engineering contract, she protests that her career demands that she remain in London. They go to Venice together, and then to Lake Como. Their lives are dreamlike until they meet a party of Californians, one of them a woman who knows Helmeth. They have to resort to subterfuge to cover the fact that they are at the hotel together. Helmeth begs Olivia to marry him, and Olivia admits that she would have done so if that had been possible under Italian law. The vacation ends with Helmeth's going to Mexico and Olivia's returning to New York and the stage. They agree to meet in New York in November and to settle things.

The New York meeting does occur, but they only argue further about Olivia's leaving the stage. She plans to meet Helmeth in Los Angeles, where his children by a former marriage are being cared for by the sister of the young woman they had encountered at Lake Como. Olivia insists that the choice between her career and her marriage must be made by Helmeth. When she meets him in Los Angeles, she tells him that she will not leave the stage. Olivia returns to New York confident that Helmeth will see her there and marry her. The playgoing season has scarcely started in New York when Olivia receives from Helmeth a telegram: "Will you marry me?" She replies: "If you marry my work."

She expects him with every knock on the door, but the Powers that she says are forever fumbling at the lives of human beings have ceased to fumble with Olivia's. She faces a breakdown, and her playwright friend Jerry advises her to leave New York with her play and go on the road. In Chicago, she has a startling scene in the dressing room at the theater when her friend Pauline Mills forces Olivia to admit that her life as an artist has been unconventional. She accuses Pauline, her life-long friend, of self-righteousness and moral superiority.[5] When Olivia returns to the hotel, she finds a letter containing a clipping from a Pasadena newspaper that announces the engagement of Helmeth Garrett to Edith Stanley.

There is a denouement. The story has a satisfactory if not an entirely happy ending. Olivia weds Jerry McDermott, who has been divorced by his wife. He and Olivia decide to wed, even though neither expects the match to be a vision or a dream. Something equally good may take the place of ecstatic love, and that is sharing a way of life in the theater, worrying about the other's welfare, and rejoicing in mutual successes, sympathizing in mutual disappointments.

## II   Revolt from the Village: Carol Kennicott

Only eight years separate the appearance in fiction of Carol Kennicott, heroine of Sinclair Lewis' *Main Street* (1920), from that of Olivia Lattimore, protagonist of Mary Austin's *A Woman of Genius* (1912). Carol Milford Kennicott is not possessed by her gift of genius, but she is interested in expressing herself; and Prairie City, Minnesota, offers the same challenge to Carol as Taylorville, Ohianna, presented to Olivia. Carol was an orphan, though she remembered her smiling and shabby father, who emigrated from Massachusetts and became a judge in Mankato, a garden-sheltered place—not the unprotected, frame village with red grain elevators and a few tinny church steeples of Gopher Prairie.[6] Like Olivia, Carol believed in the woodland gods and cried out for joy in the sun-warmed spaces of the grove at the edge of the wheat land. Carol organized a dramatic society in Gopher Prairie. When she hears the town banker remark that he didn't care much for plays and preferred "a good movie, with auto accidents and hold-ups, and some git to it and not all the talky-talk,"[7] she despairs as much for cultural fulfillment as does Olivia for the freeing of her gift. Carol found little more response, artistically, from her husband, Dr. Will Kennicott, than Olivia evoked from her salesman mate, Tommy Bettersworth. When Carol persuaded Will to take a vacation trip, they visited the Grand Canyon, the adobe walls of Santa Fe, the bell-towered missions of California. Upon their return to Gopher Prairie, they step from a wooden platform at the railroad station into wet snow and have to walk home when the only taxicab in town slides into a tree and breaks a wheel. She stares at the bare tree trunks, the spongy earth between patches of decayed snow, the vacant lots full of tall dead weeds, the ash heaps from furnace grates. Her spirit sinks again, as she measures the futility of coping with her drab existence.

Her stand for freedom and a right to live her own life is the campaign of Mary Austin's Olivia Lattimore all over again. Carol tries her wings of freedom in Washington, D.C., where she works in the Bureau of War Risk Insurance. She has no philosophy that the Powers have descended to lift her to their heights. She discovers that, in many respects, Washington is a gigantic Gopher Prairie with the same types of gossip, cliques, scandals, and view of progress. The white columns seen across leafy parks, the old mansions with a hint of mystery behind their gates, the concerts, these were the world Carol had always yearned for. But there was a monotony to Washington, too, for someone who worked in the same office, lived in the same flat, followed the same routine. Her husband comes to visit her in Washington; but, unlike Olivia Lattimore, Carol Kennicott cannot demand of him that he "marry my work." After Dr. Will Kennicott's return, she talks to a noted suffragist about her problem. The answer the suffragist gives could have been spoken by Mary Austin: "There's one attack you can make on it"— Gopher Prairie, the Midwest, Taylorville, wherever a woman may live—"perhaps the only kind that accomplishes much anywhere: you can keep on looking at one thing after another in your home and church and bank, and ask why it is, and who first laid down the law that it had to be that way. If enough of us do this impolitely enough, then we'll become civilized in merely twenty thousand years or so, instead of having to

wait the two hundred thousand years that my cynical anthropological friends allow."[8]

Mary Austin's Anne Brent (*The Ford*), Neith Schuyler (*No.
26 Jayne Street*), Olivia Lattimore (*A Woman of Genius*), and
Sinclair Lewis' Carol Kennicott (*Main Street*) have this one thing
in common: they look at things and ask why they are that way.
Mary Austin and Sinclair Lewis knew each other from Mary's
New York days; both were Midwesterners; and he was genuinely
fond of her. On one occasion, they met in England, at Canter-
bury Cathedral, and Lewis shouted, "Hello, Mary, what in hell
are you doing here." Then he embraced her.[9] She gave a
dinner party for him in Santa Fe and then spent most of the
time in telling him how poor a writer he was and in general
finding fault with him. Lewis listened to everything she said
without raising any objection. When she was through, he got out
of his chair, walked to where she sat, embraced and kissed
her, saying, "God damn you, Mary, I love you."[10]

## III  Love and the Soul Maker

In 1914, when *Love and the Soul Maker* appeared, the author
called it *A Philosophical Novel*. There are only two characters,
both of them women; and the entire work is a dialogue analyzing
the physical and spiritual foundations of love. The central theme
of this conversational essay is that love is a compulsive creative
act, which in men and women may find substitutes in art,
literature, and religion—a subject that I have discussed in an
earlier chapter.[11] However, the attitude of these two women
as feminists may be appropriately reviewed here. In an early
part of the book, one of the women remarks that an admirer
who had broken their engagement abruptly "wasn't a bad man;
he was just mannish."[12] At a later point in the protracted discussion, the same woman comments that ironically enough, "Dante
was living more or less comfortably with his wife much of the
time he was visiting Beatrice in Paradise; and though Petrarch's
sonnets were inspired by the lady of his affections, he had, I
believe, a child by his housekeeper."[13] Mary Austin's feminists
want to divide the world with men; and when they find themselves thwarted they take revenge upon the male sex by pointing
out masculine faults and failures.

The feminine characters in Mary Austin's novels are redoubt-able women. They demonstrate power and they have gifts, whether they draw from a source outside or inside their natures. Edward Wagenknecht concludes that "Mary Austin never wrote a bad novel, yet it is hardly an exaggeration to say that she never produced a novel that was entirely successful."[14] More than half of her novels can be placed in the category of romance, if the definition for this term is accepted as "a story dealing with imagination and wonder, in a picturesque back-ground or a realistic environment played upon by the freedom of fancy." Nowhere can Mary Austin's writing become entirely disengaged from her serious outlook or from her prophetic frame of mind. Yet in the novels next to be considered the author seems less insistent upon playing the leading roles herself.

# Starry Adventure

THE FIRST NOVEL Mary Austin wrote, *Isidro*, is still one of her fine achievements in the long narrative form. Early California mission days are the background, and the son of a wealthy Spanish cattleman or *hacendado* is its hero. The novel bears the name of this youth, and the action begins as the reader meets him on his way to enter the Franciscan order of priests at the missionary outpost in Carmel. The events of the novel are born of the land, the casual as well as the extraordinary happenings. Isidro helps a renegade Indian locked in a struggle with a wounded deer; he rescues a flock of sheep and two half-starved dogs that have been abandoned by a murderous half-breed who has killed their master. "Priest's work," explains Isidro to himself as he finally in his roundabout fashion arrives at the mission.[1] While he is with the sheep dogs and the flock, he meets a young lad, also a herder, who is named El Zarzo, "the Briar." Despite the youth's sharp tongue, friendship develops between the two; and El Zarzo accompanies Isidro on the trip to return the lost flock.

The murder of the master of the flock is discovered by Isidro, who starts for the Presidio at Monterey to report it. El Zarzo, against his protests, decides to accompany him. When they arrive at the Presidio, Isidro is not believed. Instead, he is accused of the crime, but the murderer in confession to the Father Superior at the Mission has revealed his deed. When Isidro is charged, the priest undertakes to find the guilty herder. With the help of an Indian tracker, they follow the half-breed who has become almost insane because of lack of food and drink during the days in hiding. They find him in a coyote's lair, where he signs a confession and then dies. Isidro is freed. While Isidro has been incarcerated, the boy Zarzo has lurked in the neighborhood of his friend's cell, having in his possession a packet of letters given him to deliver to the Father President of the Mission. Before he can do this, a woman in Monterey makes a discovery. Shaking the boy because she believes that he is a thief, she finds that his form is not that of a lad but of a girl. She concludes that the priest has concealed her in order to further his own purpose with her. Before the matter can be offered explanation by Zarzo (who should be Zarza), an Indian rides from the forest and lifts her into his saddle.

Isidro meets the woman who saw the kidnaping, learns that the lad he had befriended is a girl, and recruits a tracker to join him in pursuit of her captor. They are successful in the rescue, and the novel reaches a climax when the Indians revolt against the Presidio and the Mission. In order to defeat them, the soldiers set the forest afire. In consequence, not only the Indians but Isidro and the girl are also caught in the flames. They are saved by clinging to the back of a deer that carries them into a pool while the fire passes on. Mary Austin's writing in this chapter is superlative:

> In the shelter of the boulders, and along the shallow rill that slipped between the stones, there were small cowering things, —rabbits and badgers, wood rats and porcupines. When the last border of the redwoods was lit, and the fire roared at them from the opposite side of the gully, little dead bodies floated down into the pool. Presently there was no stream left to float them, cut off by the heat that scorched out its source. The pool grew almost intolerably hot, and shrank at the edges. There was no other noise could live in the rip of the flames; the smoke billowed down upon them, and they had no knowledge when the day passed into night.[2]

Some revelations of a highly satisfactory sort occur when Jacinta, the baptismal name of Zarzo, turns out to be the lost child of a wealthy family in New Spain. She was the offspring of a loveless marriage between youth and age. When the forlorn young mother bore a daughter, she ordered the nurse to conceal the child and take it away. However, the child was baptized, and therefore was known to the priest. The mother survived but a few days. The husband's search for the child led even into the pasture camps of the mountains. Gradually, from the herders he pieced together the story of El Zarzo, now Jacinta and the wife of the young ex-novice Franciscan. The father is forced to recognize the marriage of his long-lost daughter. Isidro and his young wife embark at Monterey to go to Mexico to live; there Isidro manages the estates which descend to Jacinta Castro, once *El Zarzo*, "The Briar," a boyish sheepherder in northern California.

## I  Santa Lucia

Only an inkling of social consciousness appears in the story of Isidro Escobar. The struggle between the missionaries and the civil government is alluded to, but the plot concludes before the expulsion of the Franciscans by the Mexican Republic. *Santa Lucia*, Mrs. Austin's second novel, moves more in the direction of her concern with social problems, but the plot is still essentially based on personal conflict. "Santa Lucia" is the name of both the novel and the small California community in which William Caldwell lives. The college, the settings, could be any one of a number of small private educational institutions in California. The new professor, Antrim Stairs, could be any new biology teacher; Serena Lindley could be the wife of a college attorney; and the Bodleys could be the financial patrons of this college or of any other. The central figure is a young woman whose first name, surprisingly enough, is William because her father desired her to be a boy. Perhaps the transformation of Zarzo to Jacinta still lingered in the consciousness of the writer. Mrs. Austin's lifelong purpose seems to have been to diminish the importance of sex in human purpose and accomplishment. She never for a moment, from youth to old age, expressed a desire to be a man; but she constantly demanded that the dominantly masculine world she encountered be shared by women, and that neither the advantages nor the handicaps of sex be unfairly exploited.

The story of *Santa Lucia* interests the reader not only in the Caldwell family but also in its educational or sociological background. Old Doctor Caldwell is a family physician to most of the community. His daughter is an engaging tomboy whom everyone likes. The plot develops as she provokes a clash between her father's helper and the new assistant, both of whom are in love with her. But the climax of the book occurs when

the young biology professor at the college marries Julia Hayward, the dashing beauty of the town, who then finds that
she is bored with the academic social pace. Julia Hayward
Stairs escapes to San Francisco for a rendezvous with a former
sweetheart. When the gossip of this affair destroys her reputation
in the town, she commits suicide.

In *Santa Lucia* Mrs. Austin has drawn a timeless but contemporary picture in Julia Hayward, a distraught woman who is
caught between the pull of love and the fetters of religious and
social conventions. The author writes that the people of the
town of Santa Lucia regarded the words of the marriage ceremony as having some mysterious quality like "blessed oils" or
"Ganges water" to sanctify the union of a man and woman whether they were suitable to live together or not. "The college of
Santa Lucia provided no course of lectures in successful living,
and would have been chary of exhibiting in its Professor of
Biology an instance of the failure to maintain his marriage,
which is, perhaps as near as most schools get to admitting that
the study of biology ought to make for successful living, even
though it does not."[3] Julia Hayward could have been saved
had anyone in Santa Lucia recognized that she and Antrim
Stairs were mismated. Presumably, Mary Austin's sympathy
with Julia Stairs's unconventional way is the type of attitude
which her mother and brother refused to discuss in the
family circle.

## II  *The Mood of Allegory:* Outland

When Mrs. Austin was in Europe from the last month in
1908 until the summer of 1910, she saw *Outland,* her third
novel, published in London. The story is a throwback to the
halcyon days at Carmel, and in the allegory of the plot may
be discovered her view of the social order. The story is told
in the first person by a woman named Mona, an English professor. She has given up her position in order to find time to write
and to establish a home at a beautiful place on the coast called
Fairshore. This could not be other than Carmel, where Mary
Austin had built her home after resigning from the academy
in Bishop. The story continues with the introduction of Mona's
suitor Herman, a sociologist. He has little imagination, however,

and laughs when Mona finds a burnt faggot and a trail which she believes were left by a Woodland People unlike themselves. Several days later, Mona sees one of the Woodlanders, and describes what she saw in the following manner:

> Though his figure was young, the skin of his face was drawn in fine wrinkles. He had a thin, high nose with a slightly mobile tip that seemed to twitch a little with distrust as he looked at me. The mouth below it was full and curved, his eyes bluish black, opaque and velvet looking; windows out of which came and looked boldness, cunning and power, and the wistfulness of the wild creature questioning its friendship with man.[4]

He is one of the Outliers, a tribe which inhabits Outland, the country of the wood and shore where Mona and Herman have wandered. His name, the reader later finds, is Ravenutzi, but in an article Mary Austin wrote for *The American Mercury* many years later she said the tip of George Sterling's "thin nose was mobile and inquiring" and that his mouth was curled. She calls him "imperfectly humanized, having the intellect and will of man, but emotions and instincts almost wholly of the wild creature sort." Later in *Outland* there is reference to Ravenutzi's "delicate faun's profile," and the identification is quite complete, for the *Mercury* article reads "George was supposed to resemble a faun."[5]

With this clue, perhaps all the characters in *Outland* could be associated with some of the colonizers at Carmel: Sterling's wife could be Ravenutzi's wife, and the woman who broke up their marriage could be the Maiden Ward of the Outliers; Persilope, the masculine leader of this socialist community could be Jack London, who turned to thoughts of communal sharing; Lincoln Steffens might be the unimaginative sociologist who was interested in Mona. Both he and Mona belong to the House-Folk who have invaded Outland. Folk like themselves are also named the People of the Ploughed Fields. Another group of beings are the foes of the Outliers, and they are called the Far-Folk, those who work with iron and other metals. Thus, the Outliers become the free and creative souls defending their world from the farmers and the factory people crowding in upon them. Such was the actual situation at Carmel-by-the-Sea.

The story of *Outland* is not complicated: Mona and Herman

are captured by the Woodland Folk. They learn of the search for the King's Desire, which once had belonged to the Far-Folk. Symbolically, the King's Desire or treasure, is Materialism, the wealth of the capitalist world. When the Outliers find it and defeat the Far-Folk, the Woodlanders decide to bury it again. Then they kill the three members of the tribe who know where the wealth is hidden. After releasing the two House-Folk who have been their captives, the Outliers flee to their woodland trails. Herman says these people made the mistake of burying their treasure. He thinks they should have used it to buy the land and to protect themselves from the House-Folk and the Far-Folk alike. He comments on the sociological import of the Outliers: "It would mean so much to us . . . to have their social system working in plain sight. Their notions of the common good. . . . The University might establish a sort of protectorate."[6] Such a proposal could still be feasible a half century later if the fanciful Outland could be rediscovered by credible House-Folk sponsored by an imaginable university without interference from realistic Far-Folk.

## III  The Lovely Lady

The mood of allegory was still upon Mary Austin when she wrote *The Lovely Lady* in 1913. The book is more than puzzling, for it seems to reverse the position Mona and Herman took in *Outland*. Peter Weatheral, the hero of the book, dreams of becoming rich. He takes his inspiration from a picture of St. George slaying the Dragon. St. George finds his reward in a lovely princess and a House with Shining Walls. Peter envisions himself in St. George's place. The Dragon is the mortgage on his mother's farm, left when Peter's father died. The book becomes the success story of Peter, in terms of his rise from clerking in the Siegel Brothers Household Emporium to a partnership in a real-estate firm. With prosperity comes his engagement to Eunice Goodward, prominent in the highest levels of society. When Peter fails to meet the demands of her way of life or the pastimes of her acquaintances, Eunice breaks the engagement, leaving him humiliated by his place in her scale of appraisal. He goes abroad to recover his self-assurance, and in Venice he meets the daughter of former neighbors, the family

whose taste and refinement had first challenged him to strive
for wealth. Through Savilla Dassonville, he regains his sense
of value and finds his lovely lady.

One wonders why Mary Austin went to the trouble to produce
what amounts to an adult "juvenile." Coming only one year after
*A Woman of Genius*, which tackled a sophisticated problem
in a mature way, *The Lovely Lady* is a major lapse. Perhaps
the critic needs to recall that the first decade of the twentieth
century was the period when nineteen Oliver Optic stories bore
such titles as "Poor and Proud," "Haste and Waste," "Work and
Win," and that the self-made man who followed David Dassonville's advice on how to acquire wealth, as Peter Weatheral did,
was a popular image not only for Mary Austin but for such
writers as Emerson Hough, Harry Leon Wilson, Henry Sydnor
Harrison, Gouverneur Morris, Booth Tarkington, Brand Whitlock,
and other popular writers.

Names of the characters in *The Lovely Lady* tell a story in
themselves. Analyze *Peter Weatheral*, name of the chief figure,
and the meaning "Rock that weathers all" comes to view. Miss
Haven, who is one of Peter's early admirers, is unworthy of his
ideal; and her name could well mean just "a shelter," not the
true port toward which he steers. Clarice Lessing, wife of
Peter's partner in real estate, borrows her husband's surname,
of course, but each of them is tied to something either "less" or
"leased." And Eunice Goodward, turns out to be, as her name
suggests, just a purchasable "reward," as she admitted to Peter
when she reneged on the sale. Savilla Dassonville, heroine,
became the "salve" as well as the "savior" of the soul of the
hero in distress.

## IV  *A Literary Testament:* Starry Adventure

The last of Mary Austin's novels, *Starry Adventure*, written
in illness only two years before her death, is a summary of her
aims and achievement in the field of fiction. The pictorial enrichment which nature brings to the eye, the spiritual presence felt
in the outer world, the fundamental truths in folkways, the need
for communal sharing, the education of men to women's new
role in the world, the analysis of individual as well as social
values in patterns, and the true relation of sex to human

motivation—all these convictions and queries are examined and
answered in the novel. The boy Gard Sitwell (who is to become
the central figure) states in the opening scene that he saw God
coming out of a cloud and standing on the aspens. His sister
Laura challenges this statement; and, when their mother is
called in to settle the argument, she compromises with the
opinion that, if God would show himself anywhere, the alpen-
glow would be a good place to choose for the revelation. There
was no fact Mary Austin so often insisted upon as that anyone
could experience the presence of God-power outside himself.
She gave this force many names: not only God, but the Friend,
the Friend of the Soul, the Powers, the Giver of Gifts, even the
Indian term, Wakonda, used by the Sioux for the Great Spirit.[7]

*Starry Adventure* continues when the children absorb Bible
stories from their Protestant grandfather and at the same time
learn the names of the Catholic Saints from their Spanish-American nurse who uses them to ward off the witches or *brujas*. Late
in the novel, Mrs. Austin states her theme. She employs the
impersonal "you," however, and the reader can substitute his
own name for Gard Sitwell's: "It was that ineradicable persuasion
of the Starry Adventure risen to the conviction that somewhere,
somehow, you were to meet with a human being, a conjunction
of circumstances, that would satisfy the innate need of a unique
human destiny."[8] The plot of the book then records the search
for fulfillment pursued by the Sitwell brother and sister, who
are joined in the cast by David Arvold and Jane Hetherington:
David, the son of a priest who left the church when he fell in
love, and Jane, the daughter of a wealthy oil man whose family
is in New Mexico for the health of Jane's brother.

The opportunity to exploit the New Mexican environment
makes possible the description of the Christmas Eve, or *Noche-
buena,* as it was celebrated by the Spanish-American natives:
*luminarias* or little watch fires along the road to light the path-
way for the Christ Child on his way to Bethlehem; the
"Shepherds' Play" enacted before the Midnight Mass; children
blowing horns and shaking rattles in the plaza; and, finally,
the crèche, or *Nacimiento*, with angels on the roof and the
shepherds watching their sheep. The Protestant children attend
Mass with the Catholic children and go forward to kiss the
outstretched hand of the Niño Dios, making a Christmas wish

when they get there. Laura makes a wish that her father will get well. Gard wishes for a star; but, when questioned, he repeats the wish of his sister; and he rationalizes that, if he had a star, he would touch his father with it and cure him after all.[9]

Gard is an idealistic boy, a prototype of the central figures in all of Mrs. Austin's novels. He loves the world of Rancho Arriba where he finds joy and happiness in the pattern of his home and its beautiful surroundings. His friend David Arvold explores this world with him. Gard finds in Jane Hetherington a girl who shares his thrill in the light on the mountains, in horseback riding, in Indian dances. Jane's family is rich, however, and Gard's relatively poor. She goes away to exclusive schools. Gard earns his way through one year at the University of Colorado, and then has to find a job. He becomes the assistant to a Santa Fe architect who is interested in restoring the fallen-down Spanish colonial houses, and in bringing back the elegance and beauty represented by their past way of life. In this process of re-creation Gard meets Eudora Ballantin, a wealthy sophisticate with a desire to exercise her esthetic gifts in a suitable environment. She has been twice married and finds men decorative as well as stimulating.

During the building of Eudora's house, Jane Hetherington returns from New York. She has become engaged to an older man, for whom she developed a youthful infatuation. Her father favors him as a substitute for his own mentally retarded son. Back in Santa Fe, Jane now has doubts about her engagement. The glamor has faded from her first girlish crush. She asks Gard to marry her to solve the situation. He does just that. "What was the use of friends if they didn't do things for you when you needed them," he reflects logically but without a shred of romance. He buys three red geranium plants which Jane carries as a bridal bouquet. Frank Marvin, the architect, is best man. In fact, Marvin supplies the ring which the groom had overlooked in the rush of the wedding arrangements. When the young couple informs Jane's mother of the marriage, she finds the situation completely confusing, despite her genuine fondness for Gard Sitwell. The bride and groom spend their wedding night in separate bedrooms, and the next day Jane goes east with her mother, and Frank returns to the building of Eudora Ballantin's house.

Neither the situation nor the dialogue at this stage is entirely credible, but Mary Austin's figures are patterns as well as people. Gard is a clean, honorable, but somewhat naïve boy. He thinks about his friendship with David Arvold in much the same terms as he does his marriage with Jane Hetherington. His devotion to his mother leads Eudora to suggest a mother fixation, meaning that the possessive hold could operate both ways. When Gard is initiated by Eudora into the rites of physical love, she too becomes a pattern: the Lilith or dove-serpent woman as contrasted with Jane, the sincere soul mate. At one point in Jane's discussion of her engagement to the older man, she says to Gard: "Sometimes I think sex is just a superstition"; and, to reinforce her point, she adds: "I think there is too much made of sex; of people getting crazy about each other."[10]

Passages in the novel dealing with the history of the house, its adaptation to women's needs rather than men's; the sex symbolism in the ritual dances of the Pueblo Indians; the phallicism in nature's topography; the expressions of intelligence on the faces of dogs—all are brief essays on topics scattered through Mary Austin's published work over the years. *Starry Adventure* becomes more than a novel: it is the literary testament of the author's thought during half a century. In a measure it records as well the currents of American thought during the period of her life. For this reason, the plot seems at times wandering and needlessly interrupted by interpretation and commentary. One fault, ascribed by Mrs. Austin to her illness, was the careless misplacement of accents upon the Spanish words used in the text. The book so interweaves the Spanish descriptive words for topography that glosses are found on almost every page, giving their meanings in English.

The conclusion of Gard's unconsummated marriage to Jane comes when he is cast off after consummating his alliance with Eudora Ballantin. He has just been another trophy on Eudora's shelf of man hunting. After tossing Gard aside, she marries an equally young but more experienced suitor, the heir to the Spanish family which once owned Huerta-Cardenas, the house she had bought to reconstruct. Jane Sitwell returns, having been informed of what was going on in New Mexico. Gard's sister

Laura has reported to her the nature of Gard's entanglement, and also that their mother had remarried, leaving the house at Rancho Arriba available for an interested wife. Jane cries when Gard explains his affair with Eudora, but she insists that this was the lesson she had wanted him to learn: that the adventure in marriage was more than sex excitement. She says that Laura and David, too, were very much in love; but David insisted the basis was primarily biological, which seemed to reverse Jane's position. However, Laura seems less philosophical about the matter than Jane. The reader of *Starry Adventure* waits for the final catalyst to resolve these points of view and to bring the obviously loving couples to express their love, reasonably or unreasonably.

So they do, after Jane rides out on horseback into a hailstorm and Gard has to drive after her in rescue. He finds her safe, however, even though bruised by the hailstones. Back at the house, Jane starts to stretch an Indian bow; and, when Gard reaches protectively to take it from her, the string slips and the bow strikes him in the ribs and on the chin. He calls her a fool and starts to shake her. The surprise comes when he finds Jane embracing him and vice versa. Powers, the Presence, even Social Consciousness seem to have flown out the window with the imaginary arrow. One wonders whether Jane still believes that sex is a superstition. Laura Sitwell and Dave Arvold, too, wed but with less intellectual turmoil.

Mary Austin believed a story was shaped by its background: "I myself, and I suspect my experience to be typical, have had to learn three backgrounds, as distinct except for the language spoken, as Paris, Gopher Prairie, and the Scotch Highlands."[11] Although she does not identify the settings, the obvious deduction from her work would be that she wrote from the city milieu of New York, the village world of Carlinville, and the mountain terrain of California and New Mexico. She contrasts her backgrounds with John Galsworthy's English society, which was so much more integrated and localized. She calls the pattern of her novels "an arrangement of story elements in true relation to the social structure by which they are displayed ... a revelation of place, relationships and solidarity."[12]

## IV  *Willa Cather's* Death Comes for the Archbishop

In 1927, Mary Austin turned over her house to Willa Cather for several months during the time Miss Cather was at work on *Death Comes for the Archbishop.* Willa Cather autographed a copy of her book as follows: "For Mary Austin, in whose lovely study I wrote the last chapters of this book. She will be my sternest critic—and she has the right to be. I will always take a calling-down from my betters."[13] Miss Cather was right in anticipating criticism of her New Mexican novel, for in her autobiography, Mary Austin accuses Willa Cather of having undermined the local Spanish culture by sympathizing with the French tradition of Jean Baptiste Lamy, the Bishop Juan Bautista of the novel. Lamy became the first Roman Catholic bishop in a Spanish-American diocese, and built a cathedral in the French manner of his native Clermont, a village north of Paris.[14] It is true that the emphasis and the artistry of Miss Cather's book are French rather than Spanish. The cultural clash which the semi-fictional Bishop Latour provoked finds its way into the book through no fault of Willa Cather. Bishop Lamy himself engendered it through his reforms and discipline. But Miss Cather's book also expresses the sympathy which Bishop Lamy felt for the poverty and the ignorance of the vast majority of the native people plus his own appreciation for their spiritual and artistic inheritance.

In 1931, Carl Van Doren, writing a survey of contemporary novelists, described Mary Austin as creating out of deep reflection, and from something even deeper than reflection, the unconscious instincts of the individual and the memories of the race. He wrote that the effect upon her novels of such methods had been to widen their sympathies and to lift their style, but it had also rendered them defective in structure and sometimes obscure in meaning. He continues his analysis of her novels as follows:

> If they are not glib, neither are they always clean-cut or direct. Along with her generous intelligence she has a good deal of the stubborn wilfulness of genius, and she has never achieved a quite satisfactory fusion of the two qualities. She wears something like the sibyl's robes and speaks with something like the sibyl's strong accent, but the cool, hard discipline of the artist or of the exact

scholar only occasionally serves her. Much of her significance lies in her promise. Faithful to her original vision, she has moved steadily onward, growing, writing no book like its predecessor, applying her wisdom continually to new knowledge, leaving behind her a rich detritus, which she will perhaps be willing to consider detritus if it helps to nourish subsequent generations.[15]

The reader now that he has considered the plot of Mary Austin's last novel from its beginning to conclusion, will be prone to agree with Van Doren's conclusion that her meaning is sometimes obscure. If we allow her to state the theme of *Starry Adventure* again, the reader will recall that Gard Sitwell had found the girl Jane under circumstances that would satisfy his innate need and unique destiny. That was only the beginning of his "starry adventure." Having found the companion, the true adventure moves on with both of them as they build their home together, rear their family, and live with the stars and the earth and themselves. The "starry adventure" is inside one, says Mary Austin. It is life.

## CHAPTER 8

# The Children Sing

POETRY is as much a way of thinking about things as a way of expressing them. Perhaps Sir Philip Sidney was confused when he wrote, sometime between 1580 and 1583, that poetry was "a speaking picture, with this end, to teach and delight." Since Sir Philip's day, his definition has been widely rejected as naïve and as really a fallacy; for in the view of the twentieth-century Neo-Metaphysical school of criticism, poetry is to resolve paradoxes from the viewpoint of their tensions and ironies. The unseen forces which Mary Hunter felt as a girl were not ironic about life but positive and straightforward. Like the world which Aristotle describes in his *Poetics* and which Sidney envisions in his *Apology for Poetry*, a reality did exist which the mind of a poet could strive to grasp and then imitate. In fact, Sidney asserts, the poet through his own invention devises a new nature, confined only by the zodiac of his own wit.

As a poet Mary Hunter began at an early age to range freely within the zodiac of her own wit. She entered Blackburn College when she was just sixteen, and in her junior year *The Blackburnian*, the literary magazine, published four poems and one prose essay which she had written. The first of the poems is untitled, but the others are called "Oak Leaves," "Endymion," and "Class Poem." The best of these is "Oak Leaves," for it contains thoughts that are repeated many years later though in somewhat different terms and meter. Young Mary writes that she is lying beneath a sacred oak, listening to the melody sung by the stars and the wind. She dreams and then sings to the oak, asking to be changed into a tree so that she may rest on the breast of nature. She supplicates to:

> Leave for all time earth's ceaseless toil,
> Strike my roots deep in thy soil,

With each returning spring to feel
The life-sap through my branches steal,
And as each twig new strength receives
Laugh my joy in a thousand leaves.
Part, undivided, of the earth
And the Great Will that gave it birth.[1]


## I  The Basket Woman

How many of Mary Hunter's later books have passages dealing
with trees? All these allusions may be traced back to Mary
Hunter's original wonderment under the walnut tree near
Rinaker's Hill. The trail in *Outland,* leading to the country of
free people, begins at the Broken Tree with the hawk's nest. In
*The Basket Woman,* a number of trees are personified and give
interesting accounts of themselves. The sugar pine is at first
jealous of the flowers surrounding it; but, finally, as it towers
above them, it grows proud and outlives all of the flaming,
bright creatures once its neighbors. The white-barked pine
longs to see the other side of the mountain and finally does
when it is cut to mend a pack saddle and rides on a mule to
the other side. Then it discovers that the slope was just like
the one it had left. The straight sapling fir believes itself
superior to its mother, for she is bent and worn. The son is
critical of her shape until with time its own great branches
begin to feel the weight of winter snows. "Droop your boughs"
creaks the fir mother, "and bend so you will not break." Soon
the young fir discovers that it is shaped like the mother, but
it boasts, "You can see by the curve of my trunk what a weight
I have borne."[2] An aspen grove is the setting where Gard Sitwell
in *Starry Adventure* first feels the spirit of the mountains. In
the poem previously mentioned, "Going West," written thirty-six
years after "Oak Leaves," Mary Austin said:

Lay me where some contented oak can prove
How much of me is nurture for a tree. . . .
Or if the wheel should run too fast
Run up and rest
As a sequoia for a thousand years.[3]

## II  *Verse For Young People*

*The Children Sing in the Far West*, the only collection of her poetry, was brought together in 1928. In the Preface, Mrs. Austin states that the songs began to be made nearly forty years earlier when the author was quite young and was teaching school. She tried them out on her pupils at Mountain View Dairy and at Lone Pine, California. The acknowledgments in the book are made to such periodicals as *St. Nicholas, The Youth's Companion, The American Boy, Everygirl's Magazine*, as well as to such adult magazines as *The Nation* and *The Forum*. The language of these poems is artfully simple, and the repetition of a melodious line is timed to appeal to a song-line rhythm. "The Sandhill Crane" is an instance:

> Whenever the days are cool and clear
> The sandhill crane goes walking
> Across the field by the flashing weir
> Slowly, solemnly stalking.
> The little frogs in the tules hear
> And jump for their lives when he comes near,
> The minnows scuttle away in fear,
> When the sandhill crane goes walking.
> The fieldfolk know if he comes that way
> Slowly, solemnly stalking,
> There is danger and death in the least delay
> When the sandhill crane goes walking.
> The chipmunks stop in the midst of their play,
> The gophers hide in their holes away
> And hush, oh hush! the field mice say,
> When the sandhill crane goes walking.[4]

H. C. Tracy, in his book *American Naturists*, calls *The Children Sing in the Far West* a book of nature verse. "Often they surprise and enchant one," he declares, and then quotes "At Carmel" for its touch-of-nature feeling:

> There are people go to Carmel
> To see the blue bay pass
> Through green wave to white foam
> Like snow on new grass.
> But I go to hear the auklets crying
> Like dark glass on glass.

> I go to hear the herons talk
> The way that herons have, half asleep,
> As they come in past Carmel bar
> With a slow wing sweep;
> To hear the wood teams jingling up from Sur,
> And the contented blether of the Mission sheep.[5]

The poet's ever-recurring search for the right word is hauntingly expressed in "Whisper of the Wind":

> Whisper of the wind along the sage
> Only wait till I can get the word—
> Never was it printed in a page,
> Never was it spoken, never heard.
> Once I thought I had it when the moon
> Stood up young and white behind the grass,
> Ah, but it was gone again so soon,
> On the scented hill I heard it pass!
> Whisper of the wind along the sage—
> That was it where once the lupine stirred—
> At the moth-hour once I heard it plain,
> Once. But I forget the very word.[6]

The early days the author spent in a "gull-gray city by the sea" are recalled in her poem "San Francisco." The reader swings up the hill on cable cars, gazes at the "gray wall-sided" warships and the gray fog drifting in. The green tide, the slow sound of the ferries, and the long Pacific swells slipping past the Golden Gate—all are perpetuated in the images of the poem.

Mark Van Doren on reading these poems thought that Mrs. Austin should abandon other forms of literary expression for verse, and Arthur Davison Ficke voiced the opinion that "At Carmel" and "In Papagueria" were pure poetry, something created in imagery that was structural and independently formed. "Furryhide" and "Glitterskin" are the titles used in poems about a prairie dog and a rattlesnake. "Dormidera" is the title she chooses for a drowsy poem about trails dim with rain and hills shrouded by fog. Perhaps the purpose in her book is best expressed by "Western Magic":

> There are no fairy-folk in our Southwest;
> The cactus spines would tear their filmy wings;

There's no dew anywhere for them to drink,
And no green grass to make them fairy rings.

But sometimes in a windless blur of dust
The impish twins of War and Chance go by,
Or after storms the Spider Woman mends,
With thin drawn cloud, torn edges of the sky.

And there is One who plays upon the flute
In deep rock crevices where springs are found.
'Twas at To-yallanne they saw him first—
In April youths are magicked by the sound.

Hot dawns the turquoise horse, Johano-ai,
Races the sun in dust of glittering grains,
Or round Pelado Peak the Rainbow Boy
Goes dancing with the many-footed rains.

There are no fairy-folk in our Southwest,
But there are homes where prairie dog and snake,
Black beetle and the tecolote owl
Between two winks their ancient forms will take.

Clad in white skins with shell shield glittering
The sun, their chief, the Ancient road will walk,
Half in her sleep the mothering earth
Of older things than fairy-folk will talk.[7]

While Mary Austin was testing her lyrics upon the imagination of children, she was also writing occasional poems upon subjects as varied as "The Burgher's Wife," protesting the Boer War in 1901; to "Drouth," a blight typical of the Southwest in 1930 or any other year.[8] A collection of her poems, classified as to subjects and types might make possible a final judgment upon her total poetic skills. Despite her considerable output in literary journals and in a number of anthologies, she is quoted as having said: "Mine is not a singing gift."[9] If by "sing" she meant only "to utter with musical inflections," or "to chant and intone," perhaps not; but what is the following poem if not *song* in the fullest sense: "a melody which is tuneful in rhythmic mood and sentiment."

### WHEN I AM DEAD

This is what I shall do
When I am dead.

When the hot wind frets not
Nor the sharp sleet;
When weariness sears not my heart,
Nor stones my feet;
When the fire's spell is unbound
And I faint no more for bread;—
How well I know what I shall do
When I am dead!
I shall take a white road
On a warm last-lighted hill,
Where saffron-shod the evening goes,
Where the pale gilias unclose
And the flitter-moths are still.

I shall take a high road where the flock scent lingers
In the browsed sage and the blue, bush-lupin fingers;
I shall find a by-road by the foot changes
Till I come where the herders' fires
Blossom in the dusk of the grape-colored ranges.
And I shall sit by the bedding fires
With the little, long armed men,
Eleheverray and Little Pete and Narcisse Julienne—
For what can come when sense decays
They being even as I, and all of us being dead—
And the dull flesh fails,
But that man is one with his thoughts at last
And the Wish prevails?

So it shall be day an we will,
With a burnished blue hot sky,
And a heat dance over the open range
Where tall pale guidons of dust go by.

Or it shall be dark, as we choose,
At the lambing pens under Temblor hill
With the mothering mutter of the ewes,
And a wind to which the herd grass cowers,
While the dogs edge in to the watching fires
And darkly the procreant earth suspires.

So it shall be when Balzar the Basque
And the three Manxmen
And Pete Giraud and my happy ghost
Walk with the flocks again.[10]

### III  *Theory of Poetry*

In several articles dealing with poetry, her own and that of others, she urged a re-examination of the impulses of expression in an effort to revitalize the art in both England and America. She compared the responses of children to those of peoples in primitive stages of culture. Impulse and response develop with individual and group motor incentives and result in rhythm. With children many objects or creatures can inspire action, sometimes in desire of possession, sometimes just in imitation. Children reach for color or brightness found in flowers and stones. They imitate sounds and movement heard and seen in animals. These are the first stages of poetic response. Onomatopoetic cries, tones, and evocative words appear in nonsense verse and nursery rhymes as well as in primitive fertility rites. Mrs. Austin cites the imitative words and measure in both a children's jingle and a Navajo gambling song. The first is the rhyme called "Blacksmith, Blacksmith":

> Here a nail
> And there a nail
> Tick . . . Tack . . . Toe.

The second accompanies throwing dice as it parallels the motion of fingers picking up counters, associating the imagery with a dove picking up seeds:

> Glossy locks picks them up.
> Red Moccasin picks them up,
> The lucky ones
> The winning ones
> My . . . little . . . dove.[11]

After the earliest stage, that of recognition, comes the stage of identification with the object, in which the child or the primitive establishes a relationship between himself and what he sees or feels. This co-relatedness of the object to the poet and the poet to the object creates an interweaving of the out-reacher and what is reached for: "To express a peculiar and precious intimacy between the observer and the thing seen, that is the first social service of poets."[12] In a general way, Mrs. Austin's

reference to a statement about an object as a re-creation between the observer and the thing observed anticipates T. S.
Eliot's formula called the "objective correlative" which he
describes as external fact measured in sensory experience creating an emotion measured by means of words. Mrs. Austin says
that, when she first began to teach poetry to children, the only
specimens she could find which measured their early experience
were Wordsworth's "Daffodils," Bryant's "Waterfowl," and
Longfellow's "New England Mayflower." She decided to write
similar verses about bears, rabbits, mountain flowers, and birds
which were familiar to Western, American young people. She
searched for imagery, sound, and movement to reproduce this
type of correlative.

The third stage of poetic response, arrived at in both primitive
and juvenile creative effort, is generalization about group sentiment. She feels that this often ties in with mysticism about the
land and with communal activities, but she is speaking of the
most elementary types of verse. Her analysis does not proceed
to the stage of introspection and subjectivism which penetrates
poetry at all advanced levels. Her search is for the basic response
to image and movement. Since the practice of poetry has ranged
all the way from utterances as inspired as the Delphic Oracle
to lines as mechanical as *Robert's Rules of Order,* a new examination might begin just where Mary Austin started, antedating
the critical creeds and exploring the earliest psychology of
sound, image, and meaning.

In a moment of exasperation, especially with critics, a creative
writer may come forth with some very telling statements. In
1920 a book by Waldo Frank called *Our America* failed to do
justice, in Mary Austin's opinion, to writers west of the
Mississippi River and to those south of the Mason and Dixon
line. She complains that New York anthologists as well as critics
know so little about the broad traditional regions in the country
that they tend to judge all books by the same urban standards
of appeal. To some of these influential *literati*, the United States
"is a country centered in New York, with a small New England
ell in the rear and a rustic gazebo in Chicago; the rest of it is
magnificently predicated from a car window." The free-verse
movement in America, she states, is ordinarily associated with

the founding of *Poetry Magazine* in 1912 and with the support of Amy Lowell; but, as early as 1904, the shaping of poetry in this form was being practiced and discussed in the English Club at Stanford, where its origins were linked by Japanese students to Oriental sources. She alludes to her own plays, *The Arrow Maker* and *Fire,* as products of this Stanford-Carmel collaboration.[13]

"There is a poet hid in every naturist," wrote Henry Tracy, in his book *American Naturists;* "and if he or she does not make verse his main outlet it is because he senses a surer expression for his thought in prose."[14] Thus a twentieth-century critic returns to the point of view of Sir Philip Sidney that poetry reshapes nature in the medium of either verse or prose, thus making a new and better reality out of the fragments of an imperfectly documented world of human experience. In one of her short poems, Mary Austin pays tribute to that group which from the days of the Old English scop to the present has played the various roles of bard, eulogist, minstrel, censor, prophet, and wit to audiences large and small, but never impersonally or without soul. She chose to be numbered in their company, as the following lines testify:


I HAVE KNOWN POETS

I have known poets in my time—

I have also known a cardinal,
A gold laced general,
A cabinet minister and several millionaires,
Learned men, lover men—
And I would give the lot of them
For any one of half a dozen poets that I know!

And I say, Lord,
When my time comes to go,
I shall not care for
Heaven if the poets stay outside.

You may keep my starry crown
For some poor soul that craves it,
And give my harp
To any angel child that plays it,

But I will take the poets and what you have left over,
A windy hill to walk upon, a filmy cactus flower,
A maple tree, a lady fern, or bee caroused in clover,
Of all I've loved and sung about just the odds and ends,
And two or three poets to be my friends.[15]

## CHAPTER 9

# The Indianist

THE LAST POEMS in *The Children Sing in the Far West* were not written for children but for adults, and not for Anglo-American adults but for first American adults—for Indians. They are "re-expressed" into English, as the author tells, and thereby lies an interesting story.

In her Preface to *The American Rhythm* Mary Austin says that her contacts with Indians began when the ink on her college diploma was scarcely dry. She was transplanted from a settled community in the Midwest to a frontier in California where a totally different landscape and people confronted her, a people that had been conditioned to that environment for unrecorded centuries and whose ceremonial life contrasted strangely with anything she had previously known or read about. Becoming acquainted with a shaman of the Paiute Indians in Owens Valley, she listened to a recital of creation myths in which the rhythms were clicked out with willow wands, an unaccented pyrrhic movement which she felt may have been like the earliest ritual chant before outdoor altars among the Greeks. Fertility rites, growth ceremonies, and harvest festivals among early Mediterranean peoples had something in common with the rites of American Indians, such as the blessing of a spring or of a field, the invocation of Sun and Rain, the propitiation of the spirits of animals killed in the hunt. From Greek prosody came the verse patterns of Rome, and from Latin poets the meters found their way into France and Spain. After the Old English period, these patterns transformed the natural flow of English verse. Carried to America by the traditions in English schools, they continued to mold the poetic expression in English across the North American continent.

## I  *American Rhythms in Verse*

Yet here, on this same continent, was an impressive store
of oral verse ranging from what could be called religious
liturgy to personal song in patterns very dissimilar to ancient
Classic models or their derived forms. Having listened to the
Amerindian models of verse and having copied them down with
the help of Indian translators, Mrs. Austin "re-expressed" them
in her own idiom and offered some to publishers. This experi-
ment occurred as early as the year 1905, when she had earned
distinction with such books as *The Land of Little Rain, The
Basket Woman,* and *Isidro.* One well-known editor offered to
publish the poems if she would admit to their authorship and
abandon the pretense of Indian origins. Several years later, at the
time the free-verse movement was gaining an audience in the
United States, her Indian poems found publishers more re-
ceptive.[1]

In 1918, George W. Cronyn edited *The Path on the Rainbow,
An Anthology of Songs and Chants from the Indians of North
America.* Mary Austin wrote the Introduction and Carl Sandburg contributed a dedicatory poem called "Early Moon." The
book contained seventy-eight poems by twenty-eight contribu-
tors. The localities where the verse originated ranged from the
Eastern Woodlands with Iroquois, Ojibwa, and Chippewa represented; the Southeast, with Delaware and Cherokee; the
Great Plains, with Osage, Dakota, Sioux, Comanche, and Chey-
enne; the Southwest, with Zuñi, Zia, Navajo, Hopi, Yuma; and the
Far North and Northwest, with Eskimo, Haida, Chinook, and
others. A division was made between the straight translators
and the interpreters. The translators were Frances Densmore,
Washington Matthews, Natalie Curtis Burlin, Charles Fenno
Hoffman, Matilda Coxe Stevenson: the interpreters were Constance Lindsay Skinner, Alice Corbin Henderson, Frank Gordon,
Pauline Johnson, and Mary Austin. In her Introduction, Mrs.
Austin points out that the first free-verse movement of poetic
originality in America had been associated with Ezra Pound,
H(ilda) D(oolittle), John Gould Fletcher and Amy Lowell,
who between 1913 and 1917 began poetic practices which were
just about where the last Indian Medicine Man left off. She felt
that the discovery of the Indian rhythmic forms and of their

interweaving of words with melodies that were both sung and danced might give a new impetus to poetry in the United States.[2]

Ten years later, Mary Austin enlarged this Introduction and analyzed these rhythmic forms, coining a phrase which was to become widely used: "the American rhythm." In her book under this title, she calls upon psychology as background for her definition of rhythm as "a perception of movement arising out of experiences in an environment." She explains that the run of wind in tall grass, the swell of waves in the sea, the swing of man in the saddle and his pacing on foot establish motor impulses in the sensorium or brain center, leaving tracks that form a mold by which our modes of speech and lilt of intonation are influenced. Such motor responses condition the stresses and releases which bring pleasure in rhythm. Even chemical changes produced by emotions have rhythmic modes, so that people are but an orchestration of rhythms produced by their way of life. The oldest poetic measure is the Greek pyrrhic or "foot music," as Mary Austin called it: two short stresses, such as those made in communal labor at the wine press and around the altars in the market place and temple. She found a similar unstressed pattern in the Indian plazas of the Southwest where the drum beat accompanied rituals danced before pagan and Christian shrines. She even identifies the original intention of *mimesis* in Aristotle's *Poetics* as an effort like those of the Indians to re-create an actual situation in nature through word, dance, and symbol.[3]

Mary Austin could not see why the "Rain Song" of Zia Pueblo might not contribute a poetic form as satisfying to the American public as an ode by Pindar modified by a Shelley or a Keats. The last two stanzas of this Zia song are as follows:

> People of the lightning
> Send your serpent darting arrows!
> Hear the thunder beating
> With its wings of dark cloud!
>
> Who is this that cometh?
> People of the trees on the six world mountains,
> Standing up to pray for rain,
> All your people and your thoughts
> come to us!

> Who is this that cometh?
> People of the dark cloud
> Let your thoughts come to us!
> People of the lightning
> Let your thoughts come to us!
> People of the blue-cloud horizon
> Let your thoughts come to us!
> Rain! Rain! Rain![4]

No one can approximate how far in time and space this type of poetic chant may be from the following lines:

> I wandered lonely as a cloud
> That floats on high o'er vales and hills. . . .

These lines are familiar to nearly everyone as the opening of the poem in which Wordsworth views daffodils beside a lake. The only thing the two poems have in common is a cloud. The Zia cloud is peopled with thoughts and serpent-darting arrows. The world of Zia is that of a people living in Western America, and the imagery as well as the movement and sound of the verses picture a world of tall pines and mountains, a blue-cloud horizon, instead of a misty boundary of lakes and sparkling water where a poet could be gay in the jocund company of yellow flowers.

In her Introduction Mrs. Austin's references to "the landscape line" reappear. The phrase applies, apparently, to cadenced verse which she believes is governed by motor impulses conditioned by actions or emotions experienced in a particular region.[5] In a review which she wrote dealing with the poetry of John G. Neihardt, Mary Austin found fault with the Western ballads written by Stanley Vestal because they failed to convey the natural environment against which the narrated events took place. His verse did not feel for "the long mesa lines, the sharp skylines, the threatening cumbres." The ballads of "Kit Carson" and other topics failed to record "in their poetic movement anything of the body swings, the characteristic gesture of their native background." John G. Neihardt's "Song of the Indian Wars," in her opinion, promised a more adequate poetic medium; for, although it followed the standard model of pentameter rhyming verse, the lines flowed on past the metered and rhyming

length to reach the freedom of a "landscape line." In this review
Mrs. Austin avers that after her long study of Indian song
poems, she could always tell whether a new song in a language
unknown to her originated in the plains, the desert, the mountains, or at the seashore. Presumably she applied the line-land-
scape test.[6]

Two years later, an article written by the editor of *The Saturday Review of Literature* stressed the lack of indigenous values
in contemporary American writing. It provoked a reply by
Mrs. Austin. Henry S. Canby was a friend of hers, but no such
tie restrained Mary Austin when a statement of what she considered truth was called for. Her concept of a native voice
and rhythm having been ignored, she reasserts it by referring
to Robert Frost's "long, undulant conversational line, reminiscent
of the New England landscape" and to Carl Sandburg's "quick,
choppy rhythms of the city."[7] Earlier, in her introductory essay
to *The American Rhythm*, she had lamented that Longfellow
had turned back to Greece for the measures of *Evangeline* and
to Finland for *Hiawatha*. Her most graphic illustration of the
thesis came in the passage devoted to Abraham Lincoln's "Gettysburg Address" in which Lincoln's syntax becomes that of a
man walking a woodland path with an ax on his shoulder.
The rail splitter arrives at his goal with the upswing and the
down-stroke:

> That government of the people
> For the people
> By the people
> Shall not perish from the earth.

With the final sentence, the ax comes to rest on the chopping log
while a new length is measured. Not long after she had written
these words, Mary Austin was invited to lecture in Fort Worth.
An eyewitness account describes how, after she had explained
her theories of the origin of rhythms, she lifted her blue velvet
skirt and twirled and kicked a Greek dance while she chanted
Shelley's "To a Skylark." She was illustrating the Greek origin
of English meters. Then she strode up and down wielding
an imaginary axe and reciting the Gettysburg address. No one
in the audience ever forgot one afternoon spent with the American rhythm.[8]

In an exchange of correspondence, the poet Witter Bynner took issue with her claim that the rhythms in the re-expressions had anything to do with original Indian cadences. Bynner claimed the support of another poet, Arthur Davison Ficke, in this adverse position although Ficke had helped Mrs. Austin in selecting the poems for the book. Bynner conceded that the quick rhythm of national life in America was reflected in "Broadway, haberdashery advertisements, electric signs, Ziegfeld ballets, night clubs," but he did not see a transfer to the quintessence of life exhibited in the poetry of Sandburg or other poets, including Austin and himself. "As a matter of fact," he writes, "I should say that there is more influence from Queen Elizabeth down through Gershwin on Hopi Indian songs than on so-called American rhythm from any Amerindian whatsoever."[9]

V. F. Calverton, in praising Austin's effort to turn the interest of American poets toward the Indian materials and forms, remarks that the "freshness and originality" of her theory have not been adequately appreciated. He believes that her effort to show that American free verse owes something to the geographic environment contains an element of truth, if not the whole truth. Like Bynner and Ficke, he doubts that there is any causal connection between Indian forms and American *vers-libre* and believes the contention that American poetry in the future will be built upon Amerind rhythms is "scarcely less than fantastic."[10]

In answer to all her critics, Mary replied that she had been misunderstood. She had never said that Indian verse had directly influenced American poetry, but that both had been influenced by common factors in their rhythmic environment. She reviewed the compositional elements of rhythm: rhythm experienced in breathing, ingestion, passion; rhythm seen in the landscape and in the progress of the seasons; rhythms expressed in movements called forth by work and recreation. Finally, she added that it is not the rhythms immediately experienced which influence art so much as those which are inherited. She then defended the stages through which her own efforts passed in re-expressing the poetry of other individuals in a language she did not write or speak.

She urged Bynner to re-read her account of how she proceeded with her translations. In the book, she had recounted how she obtained her originals, either directly from a bilingual Indian informant or indirectly from an Anglo-American interpreter, perhaps an anthropologist. Then her method was to saturate herself in the words of the poem and in the background of the place and situation as fully as her experience made possible. When a point of crystallization was reached, she gave forth the poem in the belief that it bore a genetic resemblance to the original. She detailed her decades of contacts with Indian life and testified, furthermore, that she often read her poems to the original singer and had them tested to drum beats. The final result, she felt, was a form shaped to the inner necessities of communication and feeling, both of them summed up in her glyphic phrase, the landscape line.[11]

## II  *Saturation and Re-expression*

In the matter of saturation, the notable American-English poet T. S. Eliot has acknowledged employing some such process with fruitful results. He exhibits a passage re-expressed from the dramatic poet George Chapman, who in turn had re-expressed a passage found in the Roman playwright Seneca. Each poet had saturated himself in the words and imagination of the previous poet. What transfer occurred by way of rhythmic form is not explored by Eliot although it might have been. As a poet with several generations of American rhythmic responses behind him, the act of saturation in the responses of an English poet who was already saturated in a Latin poet centuries earlier offers interesting possibilities. Of course, T. S. Eliot had shifted his landscape line to the same Classic environment as George Chapman's. Nevertheless, subtle differences between the two may be explained not only in terms of time, but along the psychological bases for poetic form outlined by the American poetess and critic. In the same volume, T. S. Eliot refers to the beginning of poetry "with a savage beating a drum in a jungle."[12] Gifted minds may sometimes travel the same track.

## III  *Indian Literary Arts*

Recognition for her studies of Indian literary arts came to Mary Austin in 1921, when she was invited to contribute the chapter on "Aboriginal Non-English Writing" in *The Cambridge*

*History of American Literature.* She called the pre-European
literature of the American continents the richest field of un-
exploited aboriginal literature anywhere in the world. Her
lengthy article can only be briefly summarized here. Central
to the statement is the use of such a phrase as "the American
spirit" to cover both the Indian and the European traditions
in order to find as much community in disparate lines as possible. Her problem does not differ greatly from that of the
critic who seeks to find the Celtic spirit in the Anglo-Saxon
literature called Middle English, except that the Angles, Saxons,
Welsh, and Gaels are all Indo-European peoples and the American Indian groups are not. From Indian oratory through the
folk tale, to religious ceremony and the personal lyric, Mary
Austin's examination of the Amerind poetry and prose proceeds.

She believed that the story of the "Poor Turkey Girl" of Zuñi
who forgot her instructions and left the festival at sunset,
thereby losing all the splendid gifts from her turkeys, should
rival if not replace the "Cinderella" story passed down to
American readers by Wilhelm and Jakob Grimm.[13] She pointed
out that a number of Joel Chandler Harris' "Br'er Rabbit" stories
had Indian parallels, especially the Tar Baby Story, which in
a Taos, New Mexico, account is a Pine-Gum Baby Animal, which
has been placed beside a spring by a coyote to catch a rabbit
stealing the water.[14] The story of Prometheus who ascended
to heaven in order to light his torch at the chariot of the sun
is paralleled in a most unusual way by the Navajo folk myth of
"Coyote Brings Fire," in which the listener learns that Coyote
cut a long piece of cedar bark and tore the inner section into
long shreds. Then he borrowed a handful of salt from Salt
Woman and mixed it with a bundle of dust which he tied to his
tail. Climbing up Fire Mountain, he tossed the salt and dust
into the eyes of the guards and thrust the cedar bark into the
flames while the Fire Gods slept. Racing down the mountain
side, he started a forest fire, which scorched the tip of his tail
forever; but with the torch he reached the Earth People and
brought them the light and warmth of fire.[15]

In her article on Indian verse and prose for the *Cambridge
History,* Mary Austin's hope for a fusion of Anglo-American
and Indian traditions is apparent. She longed to see all the
literary world of the Americas taking the same interest in the

aboriginal themes and forms that she did. She felt that great literature needed deep roots in aboriginal stock. Thus she hoped to graft an Indo-European scion upon the American Indian stock.[16] Perhaps the process is more likely to be reversed, with shoots from the Indian growth engrafted upon the imported base. Some fusion has occurred and will continue to occur as integration is fostered by the merging of blood, custom, language, and esthetics. Indian motifs in architecture are especially notable in parts of the American Southwest and in Mexico and Guatemala. Indian designs in ceramics and textiles are found from Alaska to Argentina. A renaissance in Indian painting has occurred in old Mexico and been echoed in the border states, especially in New Mexico and Oklahoma. Art impulses are not likely to succumb to automation and teaching machines. The elements that made an Indianist of Mary Austin will, as time goes on, influence others as well.

## CHAPTER 10

# The Seeker

WHAT IS A NATURIST? Mary Hunter Austin has been more often acclaimed under this identification than under any other. Is a naturist something like a naturalist? Dictionaries define a *naturalist* as "one who studies animals or plants" and his philosophy, *naturalism*, as "the doctrine denying that anything in reality has supernatural significance." Mary Austin was violently assailed when she wrote *The Man Jesus*, because she was accused of denying the supernatural elements in the Biblical account of Christ's birth, life, and death; yet in *Love and the Soul Maker* she writes that "now and then some soul comes among us, a tall and lovely shoot like the prophet of Nazareth" who serves the Soul Maker. Who or what is the Soul Maker? It is a reality that she also calls the Friend of the Soul of Man, and it probably stands for one of the Powers she so often felt in the world outside her own faculties. Is this a supernatural entity? If so, Mrs. Austin cannot qualify, by definition, as a naturalist. Perhaps then, from her beliefs, a naturist can be defined. Mary Austin wrote a little book called *Can Prayer Be Answered?* The answer she gives is "Yes," but prayer must be more than just supplication. The true attitude of prayer is a gesture of the mind lifting the individual toward some power within the created universe which is working for and toward the individual. Man is a concentration of powers within a greater synthesis of powers that are outside him. If he prepares his own attitude properly, he can rise to or pull down the strength, the gifts, and the fulfillment present in nature through prayer.

A naturist, then, must be defined as any individual who looks toward the physical universe for forces and principles to guide his own faculties as well as to direct the phenomena outside him in space and time. What has the naturist in common with the natural scientist? They both follow the same path up to the point where the naturist begins to inquire as to the agency and purpose behind the fixed and moving phenomena he sees. The naturist asks: "What is the goal of everything?" His attitude is called teleological in that it seeks to find the design or purpose in nature. Teleological answers can be either natural, supernatural, or preternatural: the first are answers in measurable and tangible evidence; the second are answers through faith and intangible data; the third are answers by unexplained and mystical facts. The scientist is likely to work in the first category of data; the priest or minister and his followers in the second; the naturist in the third dimension of understanding and explanation. Mary Austin was as scientific as she knew how to be. She was as positive as her mystical evidence would allow. To some of her critics, she affirmed more than was justifiable. To her supporters, the faith of a naturist parallels the faith of the religionist, confirming both the evidence of things seen and the things felt—even though unseen.

She believed that there were influences and powers working toward everyone through nature. She described these forces sometimes in terms of a voice heard in a place of great beauty or just in the sense of warmth and brightness and vibration. Spiritual energies exist in the physical world that are separated from mankind but accessible to it. Mary Austin exhibits a highly ecumenical spirit in identifying these forces, apparently with the feeling that more than one channel may be open to an essential resource or energy. The Pueblo Indians invoke the thunder-bird in their prayers for rain; the Zuñi people, also of the Pueblo group, call upon other bird-like figures named the Shalakos to bless new houses at the season of the winter solstice; Sioux Indians call upon Wakonda, the life spirit, to invigorate them; ancient Greeks found in Zeus the renewal of their power; Hindus name the soul of the universe Brahma; and Christians have their saints, plus the Holy Trinity, and Divine Providence. She points out that the horizon of prayer is ringed with identities named in accord with each particular environment. All seem to have wrought some efficacy if the petitioner assumed the right attitude.[1]

## I  *Prayer and Patterns*

The right attitude of prayer, she says, must begin with absolute concentration. All distractions must be put aside. The prayer-maker must insulate himself as best he can so that his meditations can bring him to complete detachment from all but the focus of his prayer. Then he must frame his petition in two or three sentences that can be easily repeated a number of times. Gestures may accompany the petition, whether by pressing the finger tips together or by holding the hands cupped as if to receive a gift. Dancing before the Ark of the Covenant occurred in ancient Hebrew times, and dancing also became a part of prayers offered by the Greeks, as it still remains among American Indian tribes.

Prayer is an adjunct to personal as well as to social strength. Following her own discipline of concentration, meditation, petition, and gesture, she found that help in material as well as in spiritual ways often came from unexpected sources. She gives testimonials as to the times and places. Group prayers, employing the same tried techniques, could achieve universal objectives, such as the abolition of war. Mary Austin sought the Outer Powers for the betterment of human society, and she could not formulate her petitions until she discovered what the needs of society were. Therefore, her method was always to search for the fundamental patterns in human relationships. She said that she had a "pattern hungry" mind, and the evidence lies in her books. Each of them could be called "A Group of Characters in Search of a Pattern." Beginning with *The Land of Little Rain*, she showed the dwarfing effects of aridity and altitude upon flora and fauna as the pattern in the high Sierras. Death Valley Salty Williams, the mule driver in the Mojave, learned to cope with desert ways as did the pocket hunter, who developed a weather shell which remained on his body until death. Her book *The Flock* announced that within its pages were the patterns of flock-mindedness, the sheep grouped as leaders, middlers, and tailers, each in a settled place for the order of going. The trusted bellwethers, rams or ewes wearing a bell, mix and intermingle with the herd while shepherds and dogs co-ordinate to guide the flock through a counting gate or away from a precipice.

In *A Woman of Genius* the unusual gift is studied in life situations. Then *Everyman's Genius* establishes that creative gifts exist in the average individual as well as in the exceptional one. Genius, according to Mary Austin, is simply the capacity of the immediate self to make use of inlaid patterns inherited from a person's ancestors, such as those stored in his or her subconscious mind. The deep-self contributes, as well as the capacities developed by personal experience. On this basis, genius becomes the most natural thing in the world, expressed not only through demands made in mural painting or operatic arias, but also in folk arts, such as hand weaving, wood carving, kitchen skills, and machine tooling. Genius builds upon the inheritance of racial gifts, and every individual can release such capacities in the proper environment under the right stimulus.[2] *Love and the Soul Maker* presented patterns in the expression of sex, ranging from those of physical compulsion to those of psychological pressure in religion and the arts. Her last novel, *Starry Adventure*, dramatizes all of these patterns in a background of both primitive and sophisticated settings. In her patterns, Mary Austin sought the answers to human needs.

## II  The Arrow Maker

The play called *The Arrow Maker* focuses around a central character named the Chisera, a Medicine Woman. In *The Flock* mention also is made of a *chisera*. She danced for three days and produced a rain that lasted for three weeks. Then she danced three more days to stop the flood! Chiseras, among the Paiute Indians, were regarded with so much awe that they were not allowed to marry. Their power was a social resource rather than a personal or family possession. In the play, the power of the Chisera enables the Paiutes to defeat their foes. After the victory, the Medicine Woman gives her love to Simwa, young leader of the warriors. She also presents him with a charmed arrow, sure to find its mark. Then because of the tribal taboo, Simwa turns from the Chisera to the daughter of a chieftain. In the ensuing action, new foes attack the Paiutes; and the power of the Chisera fails to save the tribe. Further misfortune descends upon the Paiutes with the decline of the Medicine Woman.

She tries to dance and pray, but fails. When the chieftains denounce her, the Chisera asks for the rewards of other women: love, a husband, children. These are denied her by the leaders of the tribe. They declare, "She was taught to be a Chisera, but she was born a woman."[3] The play ends when the enemies of the Paiutes swarm over the camp and Simwa, the bridegroom, uses the charmed arrow to kill the Chisera.

The symbolism of the play seems to be that the price of an exceptional gift is to serve and be punished for it. Everything was demanded of the Chisera; yet she earned only pain and sacrifice. Mary Austin, doubtless, envisioned herself as a kind of Chisera, for she experienced trials in her lifetime: unhappy family relationships, physical illness, disappointment in marriage. But even if she had been more fortunate, hers was not a happy-go-lucky temperament. One might say that she was afflicted with high seriousness, which Matthew Arnold in "The Study of Poetry" pointed to as a mark of literary greatness. Perhaps Matthew Arnold overlooked the importance of humor to greatness, the ability to perceive contrasts and enjoy oddity as a springboard to relaxation. Without it, tension promotes psychological pain. "She seldom laughed," said one of the children who heard Mary Austin tell stories when she taught at Mountain View, California. This young pupil remembered an occasion when a cow from the dairy broke up the afternoon storytelling by charging across the lawn and hooking its horns into the quickly emptied chairs. Mary Austin laughed and laughed, but this was an exceptional occasion. Few people ever saw her really jovial or giving way to hearty laughter.[4]

She took her role as a person and as a writer with almost too severe dedication. Anyone who ever heard her speak will remember the unusual stateliness with which she came upon a stage and waited for attention. "She moved with a grave dignity that was somehow larger than pride," wrote Carl Van Doren, a few weeks after her death.

> Standing or sitting, she could hold the same serene pose so long that she might almost have been taken for herself in bronze. But there was a quick light in her eyes, and her full lips now and then twinkled with amused recognition or with amiable malice. She had strong gentle hands, as steady as the brown face to which she never nervously raised them. Although she

gave close attention when you talked, only a part of her whole self was involved. Or rather, she appeared to have come back for this conversation from her desert or her mountain, and to be still remembering the higher air.[5]

## III  *Evaluation by Critics*

Henry Seidel Canby, the founder and first editor of *The Saturday Review of Literature,* was selected by Mrs. Austin as her literary executor. When a memorial meeting was held at the Laboratory of Anthropology in Santa Fe on September 1, 1944, Mr. Canby wrote:

I felt that she was potentially one of the great American women of letters of our time and that she had won the right to a prominent place in American literature. . . . I was present at the dinner given to her by the National Arts Club here in New York. I have never heard more earnest and hearty testimonials, every one of them earned—a dinner entirely free from the usual flattery and persiflage which too often accompanies such dinners. She was a great woman—also, thank Heavens, a great eccentric. For one of the roads to greatness is undoubtedly eccentricity when accompanied by a character and such an imagination as hers.[6]

Which of her thirty-five books and scores of stories, essays, poems, articles, reviews, even plays, seem likely to be remembered? No final answer to such a question can be given, but asking it is not folly. A total check of librarians throughout the land might provide some information as to who is reading Mary Austin today. A glance at the withdrawal page and the librarian's stamp will always show whether a book has current interest or at what period the interest in it was current. But such a test is obviously impractical on even a limited scale. In 1934, a California library research project prepared a monograph upon Mary Austin, giving a bibliography, short biographical statement, and critical estimates. The latter range from highly laudatory to moderately captious. In a prefatory note the statement is made that the general reader comes to Mary Austin's work with a decided prejudice, either in her favor or against her, depending upon his attitude toward the trends in American literature since World War II. Some of these opinions are:

Most of Mary Austin's fiction is dated. The revolt against American small-town "Victorianism" which she describes seem unimportant to the post-war generation of readers. The rebellion of her time and the struggles she described are almost forgotten.

· · · · · · · · · · · · · ·

Her success of getting into words the clashing colors, the mirage-like beauty of the California landscape, and her ability to communicate that curious sensation of being set down in limitless, horizonless space, which is the distinguishing trait of the American west, may reserve for Mary Austin a place among the writers of the past with an audience in the future.

· · · · · · · · · · · · · ·

Mary Austin, scientist and mystic, has a secure and unique place in American literature. Her accounts of the frontier, particularly of the California desert and its picturesque life at the turn of the century, will be of increasing value both as history and as literature.[7]

To these views may be added that of a well-known critic of the regional literature, Lawrence Clark Powell, Dean of the School of Library Service, University of California, Los Angeles, who wrote:

Republication of Mary Austin's *The Land of Little Rain* in a paperback edition will enable many new readers to discover one of the best of all works of California which, by the scarcity of its previous editions, had almost become merely a title in a bibliography. . . . Her California novels are not important. One other prose work of California is: *The Flock* published in 1906, a companion volume to *The Land of Little Rain*. It contains beautiful chapters on the lands of the lower San Joaquin Valley and the Tejon Ranch in the Tehachapi Mountains, that great traverse range which walls off Southern California. Only one edition of *The Flock* was ever published and a copy of it is one of the scarcest of all Californiana. Except for *The Land of Journeys' Ending*, a book of prose sketches of Arizona-New Mexico in the vein of her two California landscapes, Mary Austin's writing after she left the Pacific state lost the springtime freshness of her early books. She became self-conscious as prophetess, grew crochety, and lost the simple gifts of her youth.[8]

Mary Austin was always crochety. One of her Carlinville neighbors remarked, "She was the most disagreeable woman I ever knew"; but another Carlinvillian said that she was liked in the town, adding "We didn't know what she meant to us till she was gone." "She is very old, and very wise, and very autocratic," remarked Lion Feuchtwanger in January, 1933, after tea at Casa Querida in Santa Fe. "The heart is gone out of the land," was the comment by a Spanish woman when she learned of Mary Austin's death. No one can be all things to all people. Mary was never anything but herself. "It seems scarcely decent in the face of Messrs. Joyce, Mencken and the psychoanalysts," she wrote as though addressing this group. "to insist that one goes about the world with a singing bird inside and a leaping flame on either hand."[9] This statement was written in 1931, a good many years after she had left California, and her experience of beauty and her discovery of truth were to be recorded until she wrote the very last of her books. *One-Smoke Stories,* published in 1934, is a convincing demonstration of undiminished creative power; for, although some of the stories were reprinted, others were new.

## IV   One Smoke Stories

In the Introduction the reader learns that smoking and storytelling were aboriginal American ways of spending time together. A note of ceremony accompanied both, for the tobacco was passed in a community bowl and the cigarettes once rolled were puffed toward the sacred directions of the world, six times among Navajos (since upward and downward were directions in which the spirits moved) and only four among the Pueblos. The story is begun with the first puff of each cigarette and may outlast the smoking; but, since all are eager to smoke and participate, the narratives are usually short, pithy, sententious. The smoke ritual might be considered an early pattern of limited reading or listening time, a guarantee against long-winded performance. The range of the stories covers philosophy, wit, irony, and broad humor. Mrs. Austin's greatest gift was that of interpreting the land in outline and meaning; her second superlative gift was in portraying the inhabitants of a landscape, whether vegetable, animal, or human. One illustration in each of these classes will have to suffice.[10]

A prospector was hired to do assessment work in a mountain valley. He had a hunch that there was gold in the range bordering the valley, and he hated the work that kept him from testing for ore. He hated the pale sand, the sun, and the moon glare. He even hated the tree that stood above the ledge where a little water seeped to make a tiny pool. The branches of the tree balanced and fluttered in the desert blast, and it offered poor shade. The roots spread about the ledge and the water possessively, the way some women try to tie a man down. On the day that Hogan, the assessor, finished his work in the valley, he struck the tree with his prospector's pick, giving the trunk a blow that pulled it into the spring and the sand along with it. Then he left to probe the mountain range for gold. He searched a long time before finding his treasure. With pockets full of ore he started for the city to file a claim. The trail led back through the valley where landmarks were few. At the end of the second day Hogan wandered from the trail. A sandstorm blew from the south, tossing great streamers that blinded and smothered. He thought of shelter at the tree and water at the spring, and he finally crawled to the ledge of the dripping rock. But the roots of the tree had been torn away. The rock had fallen into the pool; the tree lay over a dry hole. Three years later another prospector found the bones of Hogan mixed with the stark branches. The story of "Lone Tree" teaches an entire lesson of soil conservation, as well as of human nature.

In "The Last Antelope" Little Pete kept to the same round year by year, guiding his sheep after the rains across the Pine Mountains to the desert and thence to the reed-grass fields where the antelope foraged. Two types of weapons had destroyed the pronghorn antelopes: the guns of men and the jaws of coyotes. Now only one big antelope remained as company for Little Pete and his sheep, a lonely buck which often grazed close to the herd for security. Not far off were seven coyotes, sly-footed and evil-eyed. On many an evening the shepherd watched them running lightly in the hollow of the crater, the flash-flash of the antelope's white rump signaling the progress of the chase. But always the buck outran or outwitted them, taking to the high broken ridges where no split foot could follow his long strides. There was companionship between Little Pete and the antelope. The antelope led to the best feeding grounds, and Pete kept the sheep from muddying the spring until the buck had drunk.

Then came a period of scant rains. The pronghorn's flanks grew thin. The coyotes pressed ever closer, and the heart of Little Pete warmed toward the antelope. At night the voices of the coyotes abused them both. A solitary homesteader who had built a house at the edge of the reed-grass saw the antelope pursued by the coyotes and mused: "In the end the coyotes will get him. Better that he fall to me!" The lead coyote waiting at the head of the ravine saw the antelope coming. The homesteader did, too. Away to the west, the sheep of Little Pete trailed toward the crater's brim. The antelope knew he could escape the ring of coyotes by reaching the sheep and the herder. As it neared the clearing, the coyotes closed in and the hunter fired. The homesteader found that both the antelope and the lead coyote had been killed with the same shot. Little Pete, the herder, lay in the grass and wept. Man, homesteader, and antelope are woven into one pattern here, the pattern of tragedy. "The Last Antelope" was first published in the *Atlantic Monthly* and then in *Lost Borders,* a book which also contains the story of Mr. Wills, who settled upon his family like a blight, and the tale of an Indian woman at Agua Dulce who saved the life of a white man at the cost of her own. Patterns, yes, of nature and man; and stories meaningful for both.

Indian humor and Anglo humor may not be quite the same. But the humor of a Papago woman who finally got her marriage paper from a white man after she bore him five children wins applause in both camps. The marriage paper was not his idea at all, for almost everybody else had the idea of a marriage paper before Shuler did. He called the Papago by the name Susie, because it bore some resemblance to her Indian name. In all ways Susie was a good wife although she could not write her name and never wore a hat. After her children were as tall as their mother, they saw their father driving a white woman about to look at the country, and on every occasion she wore a different hat. The white woman told Shuler that it was a shame for him to have his children living with a Papago who had only a handkerchief to cover her head. Shuler said, "My God, this is the truth and I know it."

But, when the woman went to Susie and told her to go back to her own people and not be a shame to Shuler, Susie said politely, "If you want white man, you can have him, but I stay with my children." Susie had the ranch and the children even though she had no marriage paper. Then Shuler got a lawyer who volunteered to tell the judge that Susie was not a proper person to take care of his children. After that he thought the judge would take them away from Susie and give them to him. But when the day came for Susie to appear in court, she wore a fine shawl and all the children came with her, very handsome in new clothes. The lawyer made a long speech, about how much Shuler loved his children and how sorry he was to see them growing up like Indians. Then the Judge asked Susie if she had anything to say about why her children should not be taken away. Susie repeated the question: "You want to take thees children away and giff them to Shuler?" Then she gave the judge a steady look: "What for you giff them to Shuler? Shuler's not the father of them. Thees children all got different fathers. Shuler——" and she made a sign with her hand that caused all the Indians to laugh. Some of the whites laughed, too. Shuler tried to get out a side door, and the judge shook hands with Susie. "You tell Shuler," she said, "if he wants people to think hees the father of thees children he better giff me a writing. Then maybe I think so myself." Two or three days after that the judge took Shuler out to the ranch and made a marriage writing. "Papago Wedding" finds a humorous bridge for understanding between two peoples.

The great Russian writer, Leo Tolstoy, created similar stories of naïve artistry: A Russian, mistakenly exiled, finds the true meaning of life through imprisonment; a hunter learns circumspection after being gnawed by a bear; a peasant discovers how to identify the devil when the demon refuses to work with his hands; unamiable parents continue a quarrel that their children began and then forgot. The wisdom learned is proverbial, the stories are universal, but the settings are regional. To these stories Tolstoy prefixed an essay called "What is Art." He wrote: "to compose a fairytale, a little song which will amuse, or to draw a sketch such as will delight ... the region of this art of the simplest feelings accessible to all is enormous, and yet it is as yet almost untouched."[11] In her short narratives, Mary Austin can achieve what Willa Cather called "the room as bare as the stage of a Greek theatre" and "the scene bare for the play of emotions, great and little." In creating settings for such elemental plots, few writers have found a more eloquent pen than Mary Austin.

## V   *Search For the Word*

The gift of style lies in a tactile sense for words, the ability to feel the texture, sense the substance as well as grasp the meaning. So fascinated by words was Mary Austin that she once spent four hours just looking for the right term to fit into a description, an incident related by the wife of a teacher in the schools at Bakersfield, California. When Mrs. Austin was writing *The Flock*, she returned to the country she had lived in ten years before. She visited with her brother, but she rented a room in the town where she placed her typewriter and just a table with a chair. The weather was warm, and her temporary study was oppressively hot. Walking one day from this office to her brother's home, she stopped in the shady front yard of the school teacher, saying "Do you mind if I come in and rest awhile. I worked four hours today trying to get the right word to describe the hills to the east. But I got the word—puckery—and it is right."[12]

Perhaps the word is the most primary pattern of all for a writer. In the beginnings of the American Southwest, the earliest words were Indian and Spanish. As a stylist, Mary Austin found these words more fitting to the region than their English counterparts. "A *barranca* is terrifyingly more than an English bank on which the wild thyme grows," she wrote; "an *arroyo* resembles a gully only in being likewise a water gouge in the earth's surface, and we have no word at all for *cañada*, half way between an *arroyo* and a *cañon*."[13] She uses these words instead of their English approximations, and in *The Land of Journeys' Ending* she placed a glossary with 512 terms, words covering the Spanish names for topography, animals, occupations, dress, food, sports, architecture, and religious observances in the region.[14]

Henry Tracy, in his book *American Naturists,* selects several passages from *The Land of Journeys' Ending* to illustrate how language may achieve picturing, prophecy, and realization—all the intentions of the true naturist. The reader is led to see, feel, and believe in the background of a people as something more than inanimate spoil for human enrichment and destruction. Defiled and mistreated, the earth retaliates and demolishes its foes. Accorded understanding and respect, it nourishes in return. To the thoughtless, such animism may be myth and fable. To a student of the earth's history, the lessons taught by naturists are written in the stories of all ancient civilizations—Chinese, Egyptian, and European. Mary Austin was one who read the story, traced the pattern in both natural and human history, and wrote it down. Describing the medieval centuries in which the first high-rise apartment buildings appeared in America, she said:

> Such magic is thrown about this period, by the wild splendor of the many colored cliffs from which the squared tops and ruined towers of the cliff villages peer down, that it is difficult to write it into any scheme of tribal evolution. Eagles mewing about the perilous footholds, great trees rooting where once the slender ladders hung! You walk in one of the winding cañons of southern Utah or Colorado threaded by a bright stream, half smothered in choke-cherry and cottonwood, and suddenly, high and inaccessible in the cañon wall, the sun picks out the little windows in the walls amid the smoke-blue shadows, and you brush your eyes once or twice to make sure you do not see half-naked men, deer- and antelope-laden, climbing up the banded cliffs, and sleek-haired women bright with such colors as they knew how to wring out of herbs and berries, popping in and out of the T-shaped openings like parrakeets.[15]

## VI  *The Significance of Mary Austin*

In several of Mary Austin's writings, she refers to the power of the mind to take someone away from the place he happens to be. One of these times occurred when she was facing surgery. Unable in this emergency to resort to drugs, she discovered that the recurrent intervals of pain could be escaped by projecting her consciousness into a remote blue spark where she "tucked up her feet," so to speak, and waited for the pain to pass. The blue spark, she insists, was not imagined but was something created from her consciousness or discovered as a substance, element, or place where she could go to find release from pain. After that experience, the spark of blue brightness remained as an area of flight to alleviate pain and achieve tranquility.[16] God is a spirit and breathed a spirit into man; and, apparently, Mrs. Austin believed that the same spirit was shared by other aspects of creation and that the temporal participation extended into eternity. Death was a transition from one sphere of being to another, the blue spark expanding into the blue horizon of a total spiritual adventure: "the familiar scene—morning headlands, the Three Wind Rivers and the winding trails, the sound of the drums and the smell of the orchards." The substance of human life perishes, but the essence does not fade: "There will be things to be done, and the stuff that we work in will be the utterly familiar and still mysterious and exciting stuff of ourselves."[17]

In the life story of every writer a question may be raised: how far was his life as a person interwoven with the subject matter of his books? To what degree did he dramatize himself in his work? Are the ideas and feelings of the characters in his novels or plays those of the author in disguise? For Mary Austin the problem may be stated: how far was Mary-by-Herself represented by I-Mary? As a friend of the first Mary and as a student of the second, I think that the two identities, the author and the author in disguise, are very close. Perhaps, then, the strength and weakness of each may be summarized in the other.

Like Henry Thoreau and John Muir, Mary Austin enjoyed solitude. The gathering of clouds behind a high ridge, the spread of wild flowers across a mesa, or the rush of water in an arroyo brought to her mind some fundamental principle of natural law. She felt the joy in color and movement, but she also saw herself as a part of this flow of energy. As a pattern within a pattern, she felt both a response and a responsibility to live in accord with the freedom and discipline of nature's laws. Yet to her, withdrawal to a pond or to a forest or a desert was not the way for any man or woman to repay the natural forces which had produced him and of which he was a part. Mary Austin believed that an individual inherited the gifts of his ancestors and that within him was the capacity to return those gifts to the main stream. Her greatest gifts did not lie in the social novel, however much she desired them to. Such works as *The Ford* and *No. 26 Jayne Street* are failures as novels although the problems they fictionize are real. *The Ford* is the more successful of the two because it draws upon the battles between individuals and within communities for the water resources in the West, a contest which involved Mary Austin's views about nature's design and will for men and society.

The social treatises she wrote—such as *Christ in Italy, Love and the Soul Maker,* and *The Man Jesus*—are likely to be regarded as stepping stones rather than as terminal stages in sociological thought. Yet some of the loveliest passages in Mary Austin's imaginative prose may be found in *Christ in Italy,* especially in the small volume excerpted from this book and entitled *The Green Bough: A Tale of the Resurrection.* Certainly *The American Rhythm* did more than introduce a phrase to poetic theory drawn from the example of American Indian verse. Mary Austin pioneered the inquiry into esthetic principles based upon indigenous motifs in American life, motifs based upon the European as well as the Indian experience here. If one probes the sources of each of her books, he discovers this partly anthropological and partly philosophic quest as the deepest motivation behind them all.

The books Mary Austin wrote in which she portrayed the oneness of man with nature are her finest literary achievement: *The Land of Little Rain, The Flock, Lost Borders, The Land of Journeys' Ending,* and *One Smoke Stories.* In them her creed is shaped into literary form. The reader returns from these volumes feeling that he has walked in sunlight, gazed at far horizons, breathed clear air, and met unforgettable people. Midway in her writing career, Mary Austin made a brief statement of the conviction she held as a person and as a writer. In "I Believe," the words proclaim the breadth of her outlook, the positive character of her attitude, and the living quality of her faith:

I believe that the ills of this world are
remediable while we are in the world
by no other means than the spirit of truth
and brotherliness working their lawful
occasions among men. I believe in Here
and Now.

I believe in Man and the Friend of the
Soul of Man, and I am unconvinced
of Death.

# Notes and References

## Chapter One

1. Mrs. Austin's autobiography, *Earth Horizon* (Boston and New York, 1932) is more than personal history. Into it went interpretations not only of herself and of her writings, but also of the things she stood for, her friendships, and her hostilities. The reader finds that exact dates for many of these events are lacking; therefore, the literal course of Mrs. Austin's life is somewhat difficult to follow. In return he is grateful for so much of the essence of her thinking and feeling about the world she lived in and about the book world she created. The specific comments upon the circumstances of her birth will be found on p. 38 of this autobiography.

2. Letter, April 16, 1938, Harriet Stoddard, friend of Mrs. Austin and faculty member, Blackburn College, Carlinville.

3. "Experiences Facing Death," *Forum*, LXXX (1928), 763; also, in the book *Experiences Facing Death* (Indianapolis, 1931), pp. 24-25. *In Earth Horizon*, p. 52, Mary Austin revises her age for this experience to five and one half years.

4. *The Forum*, *loc. cit.*, p. 764.

5. William Archer, "English in the Sierras," *London Morning Ledger*, column "Study and Stage," August 4, 1906.

6. *Earth Horizon*, p. 87.

7. These verses were provided by C. L. Stoddard, of Carlinville, on September 19, 1936.

8. *Earth Horizon*, p. 168.

9. *Ibid.*, p. 169.

10. *Ibid.*, p. 170.

11. Helen MacKnight Doyle, *Mary Austin, Woman of Genius* (New York, 1939), pp. 238-39.

12. Description of the Plum Tree house, comments by neighbors, and an account of Mary Austin's visit to Carlinville and Blackburn College in 1932 will be found in T. M. Pearce, *The Beloved House* (Caldwell, Idaho, 1940), Chapter I, "The Place I Lived In."

## Chapter Two

1. Mary Austin describes this trip in "One Hundred Miles on Horseback," a sketch published by the Carlinville College magazine,

*The Blackburnian*, January, 1889; reprinted in 1963 by Dawson's Bookstore, Los Angeles.

2. Mary Austin, "The Folk Story in America," *South Atlantic Quarterly*, XXXIII (January, 1934), p. 17.

3. *Earth Horizon*, pp. 301-2.

4. Franklin Walker, *San Francisco Literary Frontier* (New York, 1943), p. 259.

5. *Earth Horizon*, pp. 235-38.

6. Miss Channing's literary career is outlined by Edward R. Bingham in *Charles F. Lummis, Editor of the Southwest* (San Marino, California, 1955), pp. 172-75. Mrs. Austin in *Earth Horizon*, pp. 291-93, sympathizes with her in the marital situation.

7. *Earth Horizon*, p. 302.

8. "The Temblor." *The California Earthquake of 1906*, edited by David Starr Jordan (San Francisco, 1907), pp. 341-60.

9. *Earth Horizon*, p. 257; described in Doyle, *op. cit.*, pp. 172-73.

10. Doyle, *op. cit.*, p. 180.

11. Cf. "Carlinville and Santa Fe," Pearce, *op. cit.*, pp. 39-43.

12. Letter, November 6, 1929, in "Special Collection, Mary Austin," University of New Mexico Library, Albuquerque, New Mexico.

13. "George Sterling at Carmel," *American Mercury*, XI (May, 1927), 72.

14. From the *San Francisco Review*, as reported by Helen Mac-Knight Doyle, *op. cit.*, p. 232.

15. Pearce, *op. cit.*, pp. 86-99.

16. W. A. Chalfant, *The Story of Inyo* (Privately printed, 1922, 1933), p. 342. Mr. Chalfant edited and published the *Inyo Register* at Bishop during the period of the fight over the Owens River. Mr. Chalfant cites testimony in a law suit (Ford-Craig case) that 68,000 acre feet of water was washed into the Pacific Ocean after having been used in a power plant. Mulholland explained that the water was thus disposed of to avoid flooding the San Fernando Valley. Cf., also Morrow Mayo, *Los Angeles* (New York, 1933).

17. Associated Press dispatch, Bonneville Dam, Oregon, in *Albuquerque Journal*, September 28, 1937.

18. Interview with W. A. Chalfant, Bishop, California, August, 1939: the California State Senate on April 28, 1933, adopted without a dissenting vote a resolution excoriating the course of Los Angeles in taking away the water from Owens Valley. In 1937 some of the land the city held was offered for lease and surplus water made available, but there was no guarantee that the leases would be permanent.

19. *Earth Horizon*, p. 313.

20. "My Fabian Summer," *Bookman*, LIV (December, 1921), 353-54.

21. *Earth Horizon*, p. 314.

22. *Ibid.*, p. 321; also "George Sterling at Carmel," *op. cit.*, p. 67.


*Chapter Three*

1. "These Modern Women, Woman Alone," *Nation*, CXXIV (March, 1927), 228.

2. *Earth Horizon*, p. 256.

3. "These Modern Women, Woman Alone," *loc. cit.*

4. "Divorce Theories Daringly Upset By Mrs. Austin," New York *Evening World*, Friday, November 8, 1912.

5. Mary Austin's library contained a copy of Ellen Key's *Love and Marriage* (New York, 1911). In Key's chapters on "The Evolution of Love" and "Love's Freedom" are found ideas somewhat paralleling those of *Love and the Soul Maker*. Other books in the library were: Vance Thompson, *Woman* (New York, 1917); Margaret Sanger, *Woman and the New Race* (New York, 1920); Charlotte Stetson Gillman, *Women and Economics* (Boston, 1898); Edward Carpenter, *Love's Coming of Age* (New York and London, 1911); and May Sinclair, *A Defence of Idealism* (New York, 1917).

6. Boston *Evening Transcript*, September, date not given. Scrapbook, *Mary Austin Collection*, Huntington Library, San Marino, California.

7. New York *World*, August 6, 1917, page 3, columns 2 through 4.

8. *Current Biography*, edited by Maxine Block (New York, 1940), p. 526.

9. Mabel Dodge Luhan, *Movers and Shakers*, Volume III of *Intimate Memories* (New York, 1936), p. 88.

10. "Indian Songs," *Forum*, XLVI (December, 1911), 684-85. "Song Makers," *North American Review*, CXCIV (August, 1911), 239-47. Republished by Houghton Mifflin Company (New York, 1930).

11. *St. Nicholas*, XLV (December, 1917), 156-62.

12. *A Small Town Man* (New York, 1915, 1925), "Preface," p. vii. Favorable notices appeared in *Review of Reviews*, LII (November, 1915), 630; and *The Independent* LXXXV (January 31, 1916), 165; an unfavorable review was printed in the *Christian Worker*, XCIX (November 27, 1915), pp. 703-4. Mary Austin replied on January 8, 1916, and was criticized again on January 22, 1916.

13. *Ibid.*, p. 6.

14. *Ibid.*, pp. 189-207.

15. *Earth Horizon,* p. 331.

16. In reviewing the anthology prepared by Waldo Frank in 1920, entitled *Our America,* Mary Austin called the book unrepresentative of the major regions of the United States and said that it portrayed only "a country centered in New York, with a small New England ell in the rear and a rustic gazebo in Chicago; the rest of it is magnificently predicated from a car window." *Nation,* CIII (July 31, 1920), 129-230.

17. "Book Service to Main Street," *Bookman,* LIII (April, 1921), 97-101.

18. *The American Rhythm* (New York, 1923, 1930), p. 56; also in "Going West," *The Bookman,* LVI (September, 1922), p. 28; Pearce, *op. cit.,* p. 209.

19. "Art Influences in the West," *Century Magazine,* LXXXIX (April, 1915), 829-33.

20. *Earth Horizon,* pp. 339-44.

## Chapter Four

1. *Mary Austin, A Memorial,* edited by Willard Hougland (Laboratory of Anthropology, Santa Fe, New Mexico, September, 1944), p. 22.

2. D. H. Lawrence, "Altitude, The First Scene of an Unfinished Play," *Laughing Horse,* No. 20, edited and published by Willard (Spud) Johnson (Taos, New Mexico, Summer, 1938), pp. 11-35.

3. D. H. Lawrence, "New Mexico," *Phoenix, the Posthumous Papers of D. H. Lawrence* (New York, 1936), p. 142.

4. D. H. Lawrence, *Mornings in Mexico* (New York, 1928), p. 127: "Thud - thud - thud - thud - thud! goes the drum, heavily the men hop and hop and hop, sway, sway, sway, sway go the little branches of green pine. It tosses like a little forest, and the deep sound of men's singing is like the booming and tearing of a wind deep inside a forest. They are dancing the Spring Corn Dance."

5. *Mary Austin, A Memorial, op. cit.,* pp. 47-48; also Pearce, *op. cit.,* p. 201.

6. *Mary Austin, A Memorial,* pp. 59-61; also in *Earth Horizon,* p. 336.

7. "The Colorado River Controversy," *Nation,* CXXV (November 9, 1927), 510-12.

8. Other articles stating Mrs. Austin's views on the disposition of the Colorado River water and the parties to the struggle may be found in *New Republic,* XLII (April 8, 1925), 186; *Nation,* CXXVII (November 28, 1928), 572-73.

9. *Earth Horizon*, p. 365.

10. "Mexicans and New Mexico," *Survey*, LXVI (May 1, 1931), pp. 141-43.

11. "The San Jose Project," by L. S. Tireman, Mela Sedillo Brewster, Lolita Pooler; "Education in New Mexico," by Mary Austin in *New Mexico Quarterly*, III (November, 1933), 207-21. Also "We Learn English," *A Preliminary Report of the Achievement of Spanish-Speaking Pupils in New Mexico* (University of New Mexico, Albuquerque, New Mexico, July, 1936). Cultural backgrounds in relation to educational patterns in New Mexico are ably discussed by Ralph D. Norman in "Intelligence Tests and The Personal World," *New Mexico Quarterly*, XXIII (Summer, 1963), 157-69.

12. *Earth Horizon*, p. 335.

13. Pearce, *op. cit.*, p. 17.

14. *Mary Austin, A Memorial, op. cit.*, p. 32.

15. "Regionalism in American Fiction," *English Journal*, XXI (February, 1932), 97-107.

16. *Mary Austin, A Memorial, op. cit.*, pp. 9-10.

17. Haniel Long, "The Poets Round-Up," *New Mexico Quarterly*, XIX (Spring, 1949), 66-72.

18. Doyle also describes this occasion, *op. cit.*, pp. 284-89.

19. Letter to Arthur Davison Ficke, November 17, 1930. "Mary Austin Special Collection," University of New Mexico Library, Albuquerque, New Mexico.

20. *Experiences Facing Death*, pp. 24, 59, 159.

21. *The Children Sing in the Far West* (Boston and New York, 1928), pp. 71-72, 115-19.

22. "Going West," *Bookman*, LVI (September, 1922), 8.

23. *Living Authors*, Stanley J. Kunitz (New York, 1931), p. 13; and Carl Van Doren, "Mary Austin," *Scholastic Magazine*, XXI (September 29, 1934), 23.

24. A more complete description of the funeral and pictures of the site on Mt. Picacho appear in T. M. Pearce, *op. cit.*, pp. 208-22.

25. Reginald Bliss, pen name used by H. G. Wells, as author of *The Mind of the Race* (1915), p. 146.

## Chapter Five

1. "The Novel Démeublé," *New Republic*, XXX (Part II: April 12, 1922), 6.

2. "The American Form of the Novel," *ibid.*, pp. 3-4.

3. *The Ford* (New York, 1917), p. 361.

4. Donald P. Ringler, in *Mary Austin: Kern County Days* (Bakersfield, 1963), p. 47, identifies Rickart with Henry Miller, a

large landowner in the San Joaquin Valley. Cf., also, *Earth Horizon*, pp. 204-7, 209-11, 214.

5. *No. 26 Jayne Street* (New York, 1920), pp. 112-13.

6. Mabel Luhan, in *Mary Austin Memorial, op. cit.*, p. 21 writes that Lincoln Steffens was portrayed in *No. 26 Jayne Street* and that he had withdrawn from a relationship with Mary Austin in a manner that she felt was lacking in courtesy and candor. *The Letters of Lincoln Steffens*, Vol. I (New York, 1938), confirms their friendship, for on p. 255 Steffens writes: "I've been seeing Mary Austin ... an odd but interesting woman."

7. *Earth Horizon*, p. 301. Helen MacKnight Doyle, *op. cit.*, p. 239, says that Lincoln Steffens "ran to Mexico, scared of her advances."

8. *No. 26 Jayne Street*, p. 278.

## Chapter Six

1. *No. 26 Jayne Street*, p. 6.
2. *Cavalcade of the American Novel* (New York, 1952), p. 233.
3. *A Woman of Genius* (New York, 1912, 1917), pp. 3-8.
4. *Ibid.*, pp. 361-62.
5. *Ibid.*, pp. 487-89.
6. *Main Street* (New York, 1920), pp. 26-27.
7. *Ibid.*, pp. 227-28.
8. *Ibid.*, p. 441.
9. *Earth Horizon*, p. 342.
10. Doyle, *op. cit.*, p. 275.
11. Chapter 3, p. 43.
12. *Love and the Soul Maker*, p. 5.
13. *Ibid.*, p. 40.
14. *Cavalcade of the American Novel, op. cit.*, p. 231.

## Chapter Seven

1. *Isidro* (Boston and New York, 1904; London, 1905), pp. 1-42.
2. *Ibid.*, p. 390.
3. *Santa Lucia, A Common Story* (New York and London, 1908), pp. 299-300.
4. *Outland* (London, 1910; New York, 1919), pp. 22-23.
5. "George Sterling at Carmel," *op. cit.*, pp. 71-72.
6. *Outland*, pp. 154-55.
7. *Experiences Facing Death*, pp. 195-97.
8. *Starry Adventure* (New York, 1931), p. 284.
9. *Ibid.*, pp. 40-45.

10. *Ibid.*, pp. 192-93.

11. "The American Form of the Novel," *New Republic, op. cit.*, p. 3.

12. *Ibid.*, p. 4.

13. Pearce, *op. cit.*, p. 176.

14. *Earth Horizon*, p. 359.

15. *Contemporary American Novelists* (New York, 1931), pp. 142-43.

### Chapter Eight

1. *The Blackburnian*, May, 1887, pp. 3-4. Courtesy of Miss Harriet Stoddard, Department of English, Blackburn College, Carlinville, Illinois.

2. *The Basket Woman* (Boston and New York, 1904), pp. 121-40, 163-70.

3. *The Bookman*, LVI (September, 1922), 8.

4. *The Children Sing in the Far West* (Boston and New York, 1928), pp. 5-6.

5. *American Naturists* (New York, 1930), pp. 260-61.

6. *The Children Sing in the Far West*, p. 31.

7. *Ibid.*, pp. 55-56; first published in *Forum*, LXXX (September, 1928), 346.

8. "The Burgher's Wife," *Land of Sunshine*, XV (December, 1901), 423-24; "Drouth," *The Golden Stallion*, edited by D. Maitland Bushby (Dallas, 1930), pp. 15-20.

9. Carl Van Doren, "The American Rhythm," *Century Magazine*, CVII (November, 1923), 155, quoting Mrs. Austin's "Introduction" to *The Path on the Rainbow*, edited by George M. Cronyn (New York, 1918, 1934), p. xxxi.

10. *New Mexico Quarterly*, IV (August, 1934), pp. 234-35.

11. "Poetry that Children Choose," *Saturday Review of Literature*, V (October 13, 1928), 246.

12. "Poetry in the Education of Children," *Bookman*, LXVIII (November, 1928), 270-72.

13. "New York Dictator of American Criticism," *Nation*, CXI (July 31, 1920), 129-30.

14. Henry C. Tracy, *American Naturists* (New York, 1930), p. 262.

15. *The Nation*, CXXVI (February 8, 1928), 126; *Literary Digest*, XCVI (March 10, 1928), 38. Reprinted in Doyle, *op. cit.*, p. 285.

### Chapter Nine

1. *The American Rhythm, Studies and Re-expressions of Amerindian Songs* (Boston and New York, 1923, 1930), p. 42.

2. "Introduction," *The Path on the Rainbow*, cf. Chapter 8, Note 8.

3. *The American Rhythm*, p. 35.

4. *Ibid.*, p. 112.

5. *Ibid.*, pp. 54-56. Other passages where the phrase "landscape line" appears are in the poem "Going West," *Bookman*, LVI (September, 1922), 8; "Foreword," *American Indian Love Lyrics*, edited by Nellie Barnes (New York, 1925); "John G. Neihardt's Expression of the West," *Southwest Review*, XIII (January, 1928), 255-58; "Beyond the Hudson," *Saturday Review of Literature*, VII (December 6, 1930).

6. See Note 5: "John G. Neihardt's Expression of the West."

7. See Note 5: "Beyond the Hudson."

8. Mabel Major, "Mary Austin in Fort Worth," *New Mexico Quarterly*, IV (November, 1934), 307.

9. Letter, Witter Bynner to Mary Austin, May 26, 1930. Used with Mr. Bynner's permission.

10. *The Liberation of American Literature* (New York, 1932), pp. 434-35.

11. Letter, Mary Austin to Witter Bynner, May 29, 1930. Used with Mr. Bynner's permission.

12. T. S. Eliot, *The Use of Poetry and the Use of Criticism* (London, 1933), pp. 146-47, 155.

13. "Introduction," *Zuñi Folk Tales*, collected and translated by Frank Hamilton Cushing (New York, 1931).

14. "Amerindian Folk Lore," *Bookman*, LVI (November, 1922), 344; "The Pine-Gum Baby," a Pueblo version is found in *Taytay's Tales* by Elizabeth Willis De Huff (New York, 1922). The Navajo story concerns a pine pitch man placed in a corn field to catch a thieving skunk. See "Big Long Man's Corn Patch," in Dorothy Childs Hogner's *Navajo Winter Nights* (New York, 1935).

15. "Fire Lore," Franc J. Newcomb, *New Mexico Folklore Record*, III (Albuquerque, 1948-49), pp. 4-5.

16. *The Cambridge History of American Literature* (New York and Cambridge, England, 1921), pp. 633-34.

## Chapter Ten

1. *Can Prayer be Answered* (New York, 1934), pp. 3-21.

2. *Everyman's Genius* (Indianapolis, 1923, 1925), pp. 21-36.

3. *The Arrow Maker* (New York, 1911; Boston and New York, 1915), p. 152.

4. Doyle, *op. cit.*, p. 112.

5. "Mary Austin, Prophet and Poet of the Southwest," *Scholastic Magazine*, XXV (September 29, 1934), 4.

6. *Mary Austin, A Memorial, op. cit.*, pp. 11-12.

7. *Mary Austin, Bibliographical, Biographical, and Critical Data*, edited by Joseph Gaer. Monograph 2, California Library Research Project (Berkeley, 1934), pp. 28-32.

8. Letter, September 13, 1962.

9. *Experiences Facing Death*, p. 22.

10. *One Smoke Stories* (Boston and New York), "Introduction," xi-xv; several of these stories first appeared in *Laughing Horse, op. cit.*, nos. 14,15 (Autumn, 1927; March, 1928).

11. *Twenty-Three Tales* (Oxford, 1906, 1921), "Preface," vi.

12. Doyle, *op. cit.*, p. 211; also in *Wilson Library Bulletin*, 14 (June, 1940), 719.

13. *Land of Journeys' Ending* (London, 1924), "Author's Preface," viii.

14. Cf. Mary Austin's "Geographical Terms from the Spanish," *American Speech*, VIII (October, 1933), 7-10, and an earlier study, T. M. Pearce, "The English Language in the Southwest," *New Mexico Historical Review*, VII (July, 1932), 210-32.

15. *The Land of Journeys' Ending*, pp. 80-81.

16. *Experiences Facing Death*, p. 43. Cf. also, Peter Wetheral's remark, *The Lovely Lady*, p. 197: "where you go in your mind when you don't like the place you are."

17. *Ibid.*, p. 301.

# Selected Bibliography

## PRIMARY SOURCES

### Books and Plays

*American Rhythm, The. Studies and Re-expressions of American Songs.* New York: Harcourt, Brace and Company; Boston and New York: Houghton Mifflin Company, 1923, 1930.

*Arrow Maker, The.* A Play. Produced at the New Theatre, New York City, 1911. New York: Duffield and Company, 1911; revised edition, Boston and New York: Houghton Mifflin and Company, 1915.

*Basket Woman, The. A Book of Fanciful Tales for Children.* Boston and New York: Houghton Mifflin Company, 1910.

*California, Land of the Sun.* London: A. and C. Black Limited, 1914; New York: Macmillan Company, 1914; revised edition, *Lands of the Sun,* Houghton Mifflin Company, 1927.

*Can Prayer Be Answered?* New York: Farrar and Rinehart, 1934.

*Children Sing in the Far West, The.* Boston and New York: Houghton Mifflin Company, 1928.

*Christ in Italy, Being the Adventure of a Maverick Among Masterpieces.* New York: Duffield and Company, 1912.

*Earth Horizon. An Autobiography.* Boston and New York: Houghton Mifflin Company, 1932.

*Everyman's Genius.* Indianapolis: Bobbs Merrill Company, 1923, 1925.

*Experiences Facing Death.* Indianapolis: Bobbs Merrill Company, 1931.

*Fire. A Play.* Produced at the Forest Theatre, Carmel, California, 1912.

*Flock, The.* Boston and New York: Houghton Mifflin Company, 1906.

*Ford, The.* Boston and New York: Houghton Mifflin Company, 1917.

*Green Bough, The. A Tale of the Resurrection.* Garden City, New York: Doubleday, Page and Company, 1913.

*Indian Pottery of the Rio Grande.* Pasadena, California: Esto Publishing Company, 1934.

*Isidro.* Boston and New York: Houghton Mifflin Company, 1905.

*Land of Journeys' Ending, The.* New York and London: The Century Company, 1924.

*Land of Little Rain, The.* Boston and New York: Houghton Mifflin Company, 1903; Garden City, New York: Doubleday, Anchor Book, The Natural History Library, 1962.

*Lands of the Sun, The.* See *California, Land of the Sun.*

*Lost Borders.* New York and London: Harper and Brothers, 1909.

*Love and the Soul Maker.* New York: D. Appleton and Company, 1914.

*Lovely Lady, The.* Garden City, New York: Doubleday, Page and Company, 1913.

*Man Jesus, The.* New York and London: Harper and Brothers, 1915; reprinted as *A Small Town Man,* 1925.

*Man Who Didn't Believe in Christmas, The.* A Play. Produced at Cohan and Harris Theatre, New York City, 1916. Published in *St. Nicholas Magazine,* XLV (December, 1917), 156-62.

*Mother of Felipe and Other Early Stories.* Collected and edited by Franklin Walker. Los Angeles: The Book Club of California, 1950.

*No. 26 Jayne Street.* Boston and New York: Houghton Mifflin Company, 1920.

*One Smoke Stories.* Boston and New York: Houghton Mifflin Company, 1934.

*Outland.* London, under the pseudonym of Gordon Stairs: John Murray, 1910; New York: Boni and Liveright, 1919, 1920.

*Santa Lucia, A Common Story.* London and New York: Harper and Brothers, 1908.

*Small Town Man, A.* See *Man Jesus, The.*

*Starry Adventure.* Boston and New York: Houghton Mifflin Company, 1931.

*Taos Pueblo.* Photographed by Ansel Adams and described by Mary Austin. San Francisco: Grabhorn Press, 1930.

*Trail Book, The.* Boston and New York: Houghton Mifflin Company, 1918.

*Woman of Genius, A.* Garden City, New York: Doubleday, Page and Company, 1912; Boston and New York: Houghton Mifflin Company, 1917.

*Young Woman Citizen, The.* New York: The Woman's Press, 1918.

## Articles, Essays, Poems, Letters

A comprehensive list of Mary Austin's publications in magazines may be found in *Mary Austin, Bibliography and Biographical Data,* California Library Research *Digest,* Monograph #2 (Berkeley, 1934). However, the list is not complete, and citations in the footnotes to this volume provide additional references to her extensive writings in periodicals. Mary Austin's correspondence, research materials, and unpublished manuscripts were sold by her estate to the Huntington Library, San Marino, California, in March, 1951. A much smaller file, containing both originals and copies of letters to a number of her friends, is in the Coronado Room, Main Library, University of New Mexico, Albuquerque.

## SECONDARY SOURCES

BARBER, R. L. "Mary Austin: Novelist and Ethnologist," *Sunset* Magazine, (September, 1919).

BROOKS, VAN WYCK. *The Confident Years: 1885-1915.* New York: E. P. Dutton and Company, 1932. This is one of the best written tributes to Mary Austin's books of the Southwest, transferring to criticism the magic of her pen in this environment and concluding with the statement that she could never establish a real relationship between her world of the desert and the world beyond it.

CALVERTON, V. F. "From Sectionalism to Nationalism." *The Liberation of American Literature.* New York: Scribner's and Sons, 1932. Regional movements were an outgrowth of the new national psychology. The Southwest led in the renewed emphasis upon native folklore, music, customs, speech. Mary Austin more than any other continued to foster the interest in Indian materials.

DUBOIS, ARTHUR E. "Mary Hunter Austin, 1868-1934," *The Southwest Review,* XX (April, 1935), 231-64. Like Walt Whitman, Mrs. Austin had a personality that was epical, representative, and comprehensive. And, therefore, she could not help writing constantly of herself. Reminiscing about her career, she found it so coherent that it appeared to her to have been pre-ordered by a kind of inherent or temperamental determinism.

FARRAR, J. C., ed. *The Literary Spotlight.* New York: George H. Doran Company, 1924. Mary Austin is, by most standards, of the company of great minds. Her one essential lack is the comic sense. But there is no cruelty in her, and without cruelty humor offers but a meager refuge; a refuge moreover, to which she would never voluntarily go, for she takes life too seriously and with too consistent kindliness. She has great feeling and little skepticism. Mary Austin's God taught her the mysticism of desert sage and blue distance. When she comes down from her own standard and the desert's, her workmanship persists in all its beauty and sincerity, but her inspiration abandons her.

FIELD, LOUISE MAUNSELL. "Mary Austin, American," *The Bookman,* LXXV (December, 1932), 819-21. Sympathy, a deep-rooted love of beauty, the sense of things unseen, the spiritual core at the center of existence—all these qualities, blended and harmonized, appear in the work and in the personality of Mary Austin.

HAMILTON, CLAYTON. "The Arrow Maker," in "The Personality of the Playwright," *The Bookman,* XXXIII (April, 1911), pp. 140-41. The play is ponderous and slow-moving, and as a literary composition, it is labored and rhetorical. The piece is Indian only in its setting, and the story would serve better as the libretto for an opera than as a play.

JONES, LLEWELLYN. "Indian Rhythms," *The Bookman,* LVII (August, 1923), pp. 647-48. The Indian poems should be read before Mrs. Austin's controversial theories on their rhythms. Mrs. Austin holds that poetic rhythm is a function—in the mathematical sense—of the landscape. Really she means cadence, which the conditions of living might well affect. Whatever the dispute about origins of form, Mrs. Austin has helped to salvage a beautiful and significant body of pure poetry.

KEISER, ALBERT. *The Indian in American Literature.* New York: Oxford University Press, 1933. Two of the most successful attempts to use aboriginal material on the stage are William C. De Mille's *Strongheart* and Mary Austin's *The Arrowmaker.* Keiser calls the latter probably the best Indian drama produced in the last eighty years.

KUNITZ, STANLEY J. *Living Authors.* New York: H. W. Wilson Company, 1931. Mary Austin has written a score of books, a number of which will not be overlooked by historians of the Southwest—not because these books are histories, but because they accurately and with penetration describe in fiction, fact, and drama, phases of Western development that are rapidly passing away.

MARBLE, ANNIE RUSSELL. *A Study of the Modern Novel, British and American Since 1900.* New York and London: D. Applegate and Company, 1928. Because Mary Austin has so many avenues of thought and expression, so many positions of varied responsibility, her output in fiction is much less than her readers desire. She writes magazine articles, tales, sketches, but fails to add to her list more novels of such caliber as *Isidro, A Woman of Genius,* and *The Ford.*

*Mary Austin, A Memorial.* Edited by Willard Hoagland. Santa Fe, New Mexico: The Laboratory of Anthropology, September, 1944. Fourteen testimonials to Mrs. Austin are contributed by writers, neighbors, and friends. A check list of her works is given plus an account of the Indian Arts Fund to which she left the major portion of her estate.

OVERTON, GRANT M. "Mary Austin." *The Women Who Make Our Novels*. New York: Dodd, Mead Company, 1928. Mrs. Austin has preferred the fullness of life to the unbrokenness of a single achievement. She is, as well as an author, a scholar, publicist, and citizen. She likes to contribute to all of the things that interest her. She, Jack London, the poet George Sterling, and James Hopper formed a quartet of importance in the literary history of our time.

PATTEE, FRED L. "The Feminine Novel." *The New American Literature, 1890-1930*. New York: The Century Company, 1930. In the period between 1910 and 1930, the stronger feminine writers, with the exception of Edith Wharton and Ellen Glasgow, came from the trans-Allegheny region. Among them Mary Austin left books which were vivid, vital, and permanent.

PEARCE, T. M. "Mary Austin in New Mexico," *The Southwest Review*, XXII (Winter, 1937), pp. 140-48. The personal side of Mary Austin is presented in terms of her participation in the community life of Santa Fe. She carried on the Emersonian tradition of self-reliance, of reliance upon the creative pattern, individual as well as social.

————. *The Beloved House*. Caldwell, Idaho: The Caxton Printers, Ltd., 1940. Mary Austin viewed the outer world, society, and the personal life somewhat in terms of the order and keeping of her home, *Casa Querida*, the Beloved House. The first chapter gives details of her life in Carlinville.

RINGLER, DONALD P. *Mary Austin: Kern County Days*. Bakersfield, California: Bear Mountain Books, 1963. The article first appeared in *Southern California Quarterly*, XLV (March, 1963), 25-63. Mr. Ringler supplies details of the life of the Hunter family on its homestead and of Mary Hunter's life at Mountain View Dairy and Bakersfield. He also discovered the divorce granted to Stafford Wallace Austin at San Bernardino, California, on October 21, 1914. In Wallace Austin's complaint, he alleges that his wife deserted him during the month of October, 1907.

RORTY, J. "Mary Austin," Editorial in the *Nation*, V (August 29, 1934), 231. The writer calls Mary Austin one of the great women of America and stresses her signature in an autobiographical contribution, as "Woman Alone." The tribute concludes with the observation that "few lives can show a comparable record of uncompromising struggle and victory over obstacles."

ROURKE, CONSTANCE. "The Unfolding Earth," *The New Republic*, LXXIII (December 21, 1932), 166-67. Hugh Miller's *Old Red*

*Sandstone* was a book which created for Mary Austin a sense of the earth and its grandeur and pattern. When her major themes became articulate, they were "the totality that is called Nature," "the quality of experience called Folk," "the frame of behavior known as Mystical."

SERGEANT, ELIZABETH SHEPLEY. "Mary Austin: A Portrait," *Saturday Review of Literature*, XI (September 8, 1934), 96. The author calls Mrs. Austin the leading literary figure of the Southwestern world and perhaps the most monumental of American women writers, a woman of tragic mold and outstanding insight. Her destiny was self-directed and her choice self-made. She embodied the pioneer tradition in her life and in her writing.

SMITH, HENRY. "The Feel of the Purposeful Earth," in *The New Mexico Quarterly*, I (February, 1931), 17-33. Mary Austin turned for nourishment to the tradition of Thoreau, Burroughs, Muir—a tradition based on an absorbing love of the American land. She is seeking not a retreat from men, cities, and society, but a real avenue of approach to them. She dwells in no ivory tower, but at the meeting of all the highways of modern life.

STEFFENS, LINCOLN. "Mary Austin and the Desert: A Portrait," *American Mercury*, LXXII (June, 1911), 244-63. Mary Austin said the desert claims men, but that women hate the life there and the emptiness of the land. But the desert did hold Mrs. Austin; what she calls the "mark of the land," is cut into her soul. Mary Austin's hungry mind seized upon the life about her and wrote romance that is in all life.

TRACY, H. C. "Mary Austin." *American Naturists*. New York: E. P. Dutton Company, 1930. Identification with the land and its native mood and true-seeing through the eyes of the primitive are found in the naturism of Mary Austin. Only in some of her more formal essays will the reader be permitted to forget that Mary Austin is first and best a nature writer and a seer.

VAN DOREN, CARL. "The New Style." *Contemporary American Novelists*. New York: Macmillan Company, 1922, 1931. Whether she deals with the actual frontier—as in *Isidro* or *Lost Borders* or *The Ford*—or with more complex regions—as in *The Woman of Genius* or *No. 26 Jayne Street*—Mary Austin keeps her particular frontier in mind, not as an entity or a dogma but as a symbol of the sources of human life and society.

————. "Mary Austin: Prophet and Poet of the Southwest," *Scholastic*, XXV (September 2, 1934), 4, 23.

————. "The American Rhythm: Mary Austin, Discoverer and Prophet," *Century Magazine*, CVII (November, 1923), 151-56. Mary Austin has a spacious mind, with many inlets. Within it, she revolves and broods, turning over all the sciences, building up huge structures of doctrine, constantly shaping the universe in reasonable forms. It may be that what she lacks is the ability to focus her diffused powers and interests, however great, within a necessarily narrow field. The far-sighted sometimes fumble when they try to do neat tasks near at hand.

————. "American Rhythm: Mary Austin." *Many Minds.* New York: A. A. Knopf, 1926. Mary Austin has begun to discover the common ground for the American philosopher and artist to stand upon. All that she writes is interwoven, for she has, it appears, no tight compartments in her mind. The whole stream of her experience and reflection has passed through her and, no matter what the theme at any moment, has taken the color of her mind. Rarely enough have prophets spoken so well the language of the people they came to serve.

VAN DOREN, DOROTHY. "Lost Frontier," *The Nation,* CXXXV (December 7, 1932), 567-68. Mary Austin has been faithful to her idea of the American pattern, and she has nursed it and fed it devotedly all her life, so that under her ministration it does seem here and there to be emerging.

WAGENKNECHT, EDWARD. "Mary Austin, Sybil." *Cavalcade of the American Novel.* New York: Henry Holt and Company, 1952. Mary Austin's best work lies in that shadowy No Man's Land which overlaps the boundaries of science, art, and scholarship. When she began to write novels, her technique was rather advanced for its time. She flings her reader into the situation to find his bearings as best he can. In later years, she was somewhat given to complaint that her readers did not get the point of her novels. If this be so, the fault was not altogether theirs.

WHITE, W. A. *The Autobiography.* New York: Macmillan Company, 1946. Mary Austin had a tough-fibred brain, even though she was a mystic and believed a lot of uncanny and nonsensical things. She talked well, lived honorably according to her code, and thought strongly and as logically as a mystic can. Always we left her presence feeling that our minds and hearts had been kindled with new energy and refreshment.

————. "Women of Genius," *Saturday Review of Literature,* IX (November 12, 1932), 235-36. Mary Austin occupied a unique place among American novelists for a generation. Of her group of novels, *A Woman of Genius* was probably the best. Her autobiography is a worthy record of an interesting life intelligently and rather impersonally set down. As a novel, it would read well; as a biography, it has genuine distinction.

WYNN, DUDLEY. "Mary Austin, Woman Alone," *Virginia Quarterly*

*Review*, XIII (April, 1937), 243-56. Mary Austin's concept of folk-ness was not always consistent with her praise of man's economic conquest of the earth. However, she justified the integrity of the folk pattern as she envisioned it carried out by small communities along the Colorado River watershed west of the California state line, and in her efforts to perpetuate the Indian and Spanish folk arts.

————. *A Critical Study of the Writings of Mary Hunter Austin.* Graduate School of Arts and Science, New York University, 1941. This abridgment of a dissertation gives a general appraisal of Mary Austin's life and work, plus the chapter treating of her "Nature Writing." The conclusion is that her viewpoint abandoned the Transcendentalist system for a much less philosophically rigorous view of her own. She shared in the attempts of her time to keep scientific and rational thought from robbing the world of all enchantment.

**Index**

# Index

University of Montana, The, 63-64
University of New Mexico, The, 59-61

Van Doren, Carl, 68, 100-1, 125-26
Van Doren, Mark, 105
Vestal, Stanley, 65, 115

Wagenknecht, Edward, 82, 88
Walden Pond, 19
Ward, Mrs. Humphrey, 39
Wells, H. G., 39, 69

"Western Magic," 105-6
"When I Am Dead," 106-7
"Whisper of the Wind," 105
Wilson, Harry Leon, 36
Wilson, Mrs. Harry Leon, 41
*Woman of Genius, A,* 44, 81-85, 124
"Wooing of the Señorita, The," 34
Wordsworth, William, 109

Yale University, 61
Yeats, William Butler, 40
*Youth's Companion, The,* 104